Editor-in-Chief and Founder:
    Lyndon H. LaRouche, Jr.
Editorial Board: *Lyndon H. LaRouche, Jr. , Helga Zepp-LaRouche, Robert Ingraham, Tony Papert, Gerald Rose, Dennis Small, Jeffrey Steinberg, William Wertz*
Co-Editors: *Robert Ingraham, Tony Papert*
Managing Editor: *Nancy Spannaus*
Technology: *Marsha Freeman*
Books: *Katherine Notley*
Ebooks: *Richard Burden*
Graphics: *Alan Yue*
Photos: *Stuart Lewis*
Circulation Manager: *Stanley Ezrol*

INTELLIGENCE DIRECTORS
Counterintelligence: *Jeffrey Steinberg, Michele Steinberg*
Economics: *John Hoefle, Marcia Merry Baker, Paul Gallagher*
History: *Anton Chaitkin*
Ibero-America: *Dennis Small*
Russia and Eastern Europe: *Rachel Douglas*
United States: *Debra Freeman*

INTERNATIONAL BUREAUS
Bogotá: *Miriam Redondo*
Berlin: *Rainer Apel*
Copenhagen: *Tom Gillesberg*
Houston: *Harley Schlanger*
Lima: *Sara Madueño*
Melbourne: *Robert Barwick*
Mexico City: *Gerardo Castilleja Chávez*
New Delhi: *Ramtanu Maitra*
Paris: *Christine Bierre*
Stockholm: *Ulf Sandmark*
United Nations, N.Y.C.: *Leni Rubinstein*
Washington, D.C.: *William Jones*
Wiesbaden: *Göran Haglund*

ON THE WEB
e-mail: eirns@larouchepub.com
www.larouchepub.com
www.executiveintelligencereview.com
www.larouchepub.com/eiw
Webmaster: *John Sigerson*
Assistant Webmaster: *George Hollis*
Editor, Arabic-language edition: *Hussein Askary*

EIR (ISSN 0273-6314) *is published weekly (50 issues), by EIR News Service, Inc., P.O. Box 17390, Washington, D.C. 20041-0390. (703) 297-8434*

European Headquarters: E.I.R. GmbH, Postfach Bahnstrasse 9a, D-65205, Wiesbaden, Germany
Tel: 49-611-73650
Homepage: http://www.eir.de
e-mail: info@eir.de
Director: Georg Neudecker

Montreal, Canada: 514-461-1557
eir@eircanada.ca

Denmark: EIR - Denmark, Sankt Knuds Vej 11, basement left, DK-1903 Frederiksberg, Denmark.
Tel.: +45 35 43 60 40, Fax: +45 35 43 87 57. e-mail: eirdk@hotmail.com.

Mexico City: EIR, Sor Juana Inés de la Cruz 242-2 Col. Agricultura C.P. 11360 Delegación M. Hidalgo, México D.F.
Tel. (5525) 5318-2301
eirmexico@gmail.com

Copyright: ©2017 EIR News Service. All rights reserved. Reproduction in whole or in part without permission strictly prohibited.

Canada Post Publication Sales Agreement #40683579

Postmaster: Send all address changes to *EIR*, P.O. Box 17390, Washington, D.C. 20041-0390.

Signed articles in *EIR* represent the views of the authors, and not necessarily those of the Editorial Board.

A Call to Leadership

Kesha Rogers Declares Her Independent Bid for The 9th CD of Texas

On Dec. 7, Kesha Rogers announced her candidacy as an Independent for the 9th Congressional District of Texas, held since 2005 by Democratic Congressman Al Green. The 9th CD serves almost 800,000 in the southwestern portion of the greater Houston area. In a video statement announcing her campaign, Rogers calls out Representative Green's recent resolution to impeach President Trump as grandstanding, and doing nothing to address the true needs or interests of the people of the 9th District. In an interview today, Rogers sketched the main planks of her campaign as follows:

There has been no real economic upturn in the lives of many of the people of the 9th District since the 2008 financial collapse, and many in the District remain trapped in brutal poverty, gang violence, and drugs. On the national level, Wall Street has continued the same policies which led to the 2008 collapse and, throughout the world, those in the know behind closed doors, whisper that another collapse is imminent. We continue to suffer from the neglect of necessary infrastructure which created the tragedy known as Hurri-

Kesha Rogers

cane Harvey. We are provided no compelling vision of the future, and the necessary scientific and other forms of education which must accompany that, for our youth.

Around the world in China, an entirely different perspective for the future is being brought into being by the great One Belt One Road project, the largest infrastructure project ever undertaken by mankind. Whole new cities are being engineered and built. High speed rail takes citizens across great distances in minimal times. Manufacturing is accomplished on modern platforms. Space exploration has been made a priority. Most importantly, the people are optimistic about the future; new ideas are the subject of impassioned debate and discussion.

This is a project long envisioned and campaigned for by Lyndon and Helga LaRouche. President Trump, who Congressman Green wants to impeach, is exploring how the United States can benefit from this Great Project. West Virginia, for example, has just received an $83.7 billion investment package as the result of President Trump's negotiations with his friend, President Xi Jinping. Houston's Mayor has also recently traveled to China seeking similar types of investment.

I am announcing my candidacy for the 9th CD of Texas to provide leadership and address needed solutions to the problems faced not just by the citizens of this district, but by the nation as a whole. Many of you know that this is the reason for my past campaigns and why I achieved significant number of votes in winning two primaries for Congress and forcing a runoff in a U.S. Senate Campaign. I stood for the space program that President Obama abandoned. I stood for fundamental investment in building the cities and infrastructure of the future. I stood for reintroducing science, classical forms of music and culture, and putting discovery into the education of our young people. I stood for figuring out how to create a new human renaissance to ensure that all citizens will have productive jobs. Nobody presently in Washington is articulating anything near the solutions we need or, worse, they continue the same failed policies of endless war, economic bailouts, and partisan gridlock. Nobody in the U.S. Congress in either party is articulating a positive vision for the position of the United States in the world.

The time has come for someone to step forward and declare that the U.S.A. must join with the international Belt and Road Initiative led by China, and launch a bold new era of rapid scientific and cultural advance—a new era that puts our people back to work, and builds up a future we can be proud of right here. As a Congresswoman, I will be uniquely situated to carry this fight to Washington, D.C. to ensure that my constituents can be optimistic once again, as they create a better future. That is why I am announcing my candidacy as an independent for the 9th Congressional District—to provide a voice of sanity and optimism for the future, over the screams and wails of party hacks in their indefensible failure before the American people.

EIR Contents

www.larouchepub.com Volume 44, Number 50, December 15, 2017

Cover This Week

Kesha Rogers.

EIRNS/Stuart Lewis

A CALL TO LEADERSHIP

2 EDITORIAL
Kesha Rogers Declares Her Independent Bid for the 9th CD of Texas

I. The New System of the World

5 ZEPP-LAROUCHE WEBCAST
As the Pace Quickens for the World Land-Bridge, Mueller Must Go!

12 **The Spirit of the New Silk Road Captures the World**
by Mike Billington

21 GUEST ARTICLE: DAISUKE KOTEGAWA
Financial Capitalism and the Future

24 **Enormous West Virginia-China Energy Deal Is a 'Win-Win' Economic Paradigm for the U.S.A.**
by Timothy Rush

27 **Press Conference: West Virginia Gov. Jim Justice**

II. The Science of Strategy

28 BOSTON SCHILLER INSTITUTE MEETING
Friedrich Schiller, Confucius, and the Spirit of the New Silk Road

29 WILLIAM FERGUSON
The Spirit of the New Silk Road

33 HOW TO DEFEAT THE BRITISH COUP AGAINST TRUMP
Apply the Flank of the Mind over the Next 52 Days

43 A TIMELINE AND KEY PLAYERS
British Intervention into 2016 U.S. Election

III. Uncorrupting the Roots of Science

45 MORE ON PHYSICAL TIME
The Meaning of Physical Time
by Lyndon H. LaRouche, Jr.
February 3, 2009

57 EDITORIAL
Awakening the True America: Who Are the Coup Plotters Really?
by Michael G. Steger

ZEPP-LAROUCHE WEBCAST

As the Pace Quickens for the World Land-Bridge, Mueller Must Go!

This is an edited transcriipt of the Dec. 7 webcast of Helga Zepp-LaRouche, available at http://newparadigm.schillerinstitute.com

Harley Schlanger: Hello, I'm Harley Schlanger from the Schiller Institute. Welcome to this week's strategic briefing from the Schiller Institute founder and President Helga Zepp-LaRouche. Since we did not have a webcast last week, there's a lot of news to get to, and let me start with what I think is one of the most important events that took place, which was on Nov. 25-26 in Bad Soden, Germany, just outside of Frankfurt, when the Schiller Institute held an international conference under the title of "Fulfilling the Dream of Mankind," a discussion of the broad implications of the New Silk Road and the New Paradigm. There was a large audience representing more than 30 nations, a number of key presentations, a lot of discussion, and videos of this are available on the New Paradigm Schiller Institute website: http://newparadigm.schillerinstitute.com/fulfilling-dream-mankind/. I'd urge people to take some time to look at them and study them. [Also see Dec. 1 and Dec. 8 issues of *EIR*.]

One of the key events at that, was the keynote given by Helga. And Helga, I thought this was an extraordinary conference, and I'd like to get your thoughts on it.

Helga Zepp-LaRouche: I think so too, and I also got similar responses from many of the participants. Because, if you look at the perspective which we laid

EIRNS/Christopher Lewis

Helga Zepp-LaRouche (right) with participants at the Nov. 25-26 Schiller Institute Conference in Bad Soden/Taunus, Germany.

out at this conference, both the strategic significance of the New Silk Road strategically and the unbelievable dynamic that initiative is taking, but also, we have a very specific focus, namely the development of Africa and the development of Southwest Asia—the reconstruction of the countries of the Middle East. Now that there is a possibility that the war is coming to an end with the defeat of ISIS, the reconstruction of Syria can begin, and the New Silk Road can also be extended into Iraq, possibly Afghanistan—and hopefully soon, the terrible situation in Yemen can also be addressed by real economic development, which obviously is extremely urgent.

But if you look at the plans we laid out, we had very high-level speakers from China, from Egypt, from the

United States, and from many countries in Eurasia. We had a whole section on the development of the Balkan countries; so I think this conference really was in absolute, stark contrast to the absence of any kind of a vision in the so-called "coalition" discussions in Berlin. Also if you look at the miserable result of the meeting between the European Union and the African Union in Ivory Coast, which took place more or less at the same time, which resulted in absolutely no perspective—I think it makes really very urgent that we continue the mobilization to get the European nations into collaboration with the New Silk Road of China.

The conference was really very, very uplifting and made people extremely happy. We published a new study by the Schiller Institute, called *Extending the New Silk Road to Southwest Asia and Africa*. This is a very comprehensive study, which I would suggest everybody who is interested in the development of Africa or of the Middle East should get. It's also a perfect Christmas gift, much more productive than video games or play stations, because it pertains to the real future of how mankind can get out of this crisis.

I think this conference was groundbreaking, and I would encourage you, our viewers, visitors, and listeners, to go to this website, and just take the time to listen to the speeches, because you will see there is a perspective for how we can move Africa into a completely new paradigm, and I think the time is just right for this to happen.

I just saw a beautiful speech by the President of Ghana, Nana Akufo-Addo, who on the occasion of the visit of French President Emmanuel Macron to his country, in an absolutely self-confident speech, stated that the African nations no longer want to be at the mercy of Europeans, but that they want to take their own fate into their own hands. This represents a completely new self-confidence of in Africa. Therefore the perspective we discussed at our conference finds very, very fertile ground right now: Because Africans are

Press conference by the Presidents of Ghana and France in Accra

25:01 / 29:08

Connected Africa

Ghana President Nana Addo Dankwa Akufo-Addo (right podium) in a joint press conference Dec. 3, 2017, in Accra, Ghana, with the President of France, Emmanuel Macron (left podium).

sick and tired of being sidelined by the IMF conditionalities or the World Bank; and because of the Chinese investments, especially in the last ten years, but especially the last four years, there is a new confidence that Africa can overcome its underdevelopment. The President of Ghana just said it: He said, the energy which the young people of Africa are now using to cross the Sahara, and to cross the Mediterranean in tiny boats, risking their lives—that energy should be redirected for the building up of Ghana and all the other nations of Africa.

I think there is a new spirit, and whoever is concerned about the refugee crisis or the fate of Africa—or the fate of Europe, for that matter—should get our study and get onboard with the Schiller Institute to help us to get European nations onto a different perspective.

Schlanger: I think one of the more interesting parts of that exchange between the President of Ghana, Nana Akufo-Addo, and Macron was the look on Macron's face; because many African leaders have been saying such things privately, but what you're talking about as this new self-confidence, is the ability to express it publicly in a forum like that, and to say, "Look, we don't want you to come here and be our sugardaddies. We're going to build and this is our future." And I think that was something that was clear at our conference.

Right after our conference, you took a trip to China

Helga Zepp-LaRouche spoke at this 21st Century Maritime Silk Road Forum, Nov. 29, in Zhuhai, Guangdong, China.

EIRNS

where you participated in a conference on the Maritime Silk Road, and I thought it was interesting that in your speech, you continued the theme of your keynote in Bad Soden of the dialogue among cultures, throughout the world and across the centuries, starting with Confucius. How was your presentation received by the audience in China?

Zepp-LaRouche: I think it was received extremely well. I would have liked to speak about the economic part of the New Silk Road, but they wanted me to explicitly talk about the cultural exchange. I think that everybody really responded to the idea that you have to go to the best tradition of each culture and each nation, and then have a dialogue among them on that level.

I must say a couple of words about my experience. It's not the first time that I was in the province of Guangdong. The conference took place in Zhuhai, which is near the southern tip of Guangdong, just next to Macau and opposite Hong Kong. I was really, absolutely, impressed: This region of China has undertaken a development which is absolutely breathtaking, in terms of new industries and new city planning. We visited, as part of the conference proceedings, a city-planning center, where in a very, very impressive way they portrayed how all the modular aspects of the city of Zhuhai were composed in the best possible way, connecting population areas, living quarters, industrial areas, and research centers. This was really, as one of the visitors said, "city-planning at its best—that is exactly how you should plan a city."

For me, the absolute high point, was traveling over the new sea bridge which is the largest sea bridge in China: It's 55 km, and it connects Zhuhai, Macao, and Hong Kong. We came to within about 17 km from Hong Kong. It is really a total masterpiece of engineering. They had to invent 120 new patented techniques to build this bridge. For example, it has tunnels and artificial islands, and some of the area of the underground is very soft, so they had to develop new techniques to drive cylinders into the ground. It was just incredible. It took them only eight years to build this unbelievable, very, very beautiful and modern bridge.

Construction site of the main bridge parts of the Hong Kong-Zhuhai-Macao Bridge.

Xinhua/Liang Xu

Helga Zepp-LaRouche was a speaker at the forum in Zhuhai.

And if you compare that, for example, with the abysmally slow speed at which even reconstruction of the highways is being done in Germany or elsewhere, it really shows that the New Silk Road Spirit and the idea of the Chinese economic miracle—you know, it is something which used to be German, which used to be the German economic miracle, but people here have forgotten that. And when here you travel on a German highway, you see two people working for five days a week, and most of the time no work occurs, but incredible traffic jams happen. I think we need a completely new view on how we build things, on how we reconstruct our infrastructure. Really we can learn a lot from the Chinese right now.

I was really impressed. You now have an unbelievable number of conferences about the New Silk Road! In Latin America, one took place in Uruguay, with 3,000 people from Caribbean countries and Latin American countries. You had the 16+1 conference in Budapest. I don't want to name all of them, but you have practically a huge conference almost every day somewhere in the world. This dynamic is really moving quickly. It is almost incomprehensible why some people in Berlin and in Brussels are still dragging their feet the way they do. They should give this up and join the New Paradigm!

What's Behind 'Russiagate'?

Schlanger: And of course, we have the same problem in Washington. If you look at the press in the trans-Atlantic region, the kind of report that you just gave, of optimism, of growth, of a real dynamic—there's no sense of that. People are still stuck in the 1970s or 1980s, in their view of Russia and of China. That's got to change.

You mentioned all these conferences taking place. At the same time, We have the absurdity of Joe Biden writing an article in *Foreign Affairs* magazine, pushing the Hillary Clinton/Obama line that Russia is the great threat. The International Olympic Committee, in a totally spiteful way, kicked Russia out of the Winter Olympics! This kind of mentality, again, shows the Cold War spirit, as opposed to the spirit of the New Silk Road.

That, of course, is what dominates the whole Mueller investigation into Trump. I'd like you discuss that, because I think people really have to get a sense that this investigation is falling apart. Trump tweeted out this week, something like "It all starts to make sense," regarding revelations concerning this character Peter Strzok.

Helga, I know you've been following this. The important news that people aren't getting, is that the FBI, *from the beginning* was part of the buildup of this narrative of "Russia did it, Putin did it." It went through top levels of the FBI; Strzok was the number-two guy in counterintelligence. He was in on the interview with Hillary Clinton, the interview with Flynn that led to his guilty plea.

Put this together for us, because you just gave a picture of this dynamic in Eurasia, while in the West we're heading toward a financial collapse, and a political disintegration as well.

Zepp-LaRouche: We should remind ourselves that the whole purpose of Russiagate has nothing to do with Russia meddling in the U.S. elections, or anything like that. It was entirely an operation to prevent President Trump from having a positive relationship with Russia. Also with China, after he changed his line on China, which was still very anti-China during the election campaign, but after he met President Xi Jinping in Mar-a-Lago in April, that completely changed. They have developed a very good relationship ever since. The whole operation came through the FBI and the Department of Justice, which is still full of people from the Obama/Hillary Clinton clan, in collusion with British intelligence. They set up all kinds of operations in order to box Trump in, so that he couldn't carry out any of his foreign policy aims.

Now it turns out, this Peter Strzok was involved in the investigation of Hillary Clinton and her use of a private server for emails. And he changed the language in the report from "gross negligence" to "extremely careless." The difference in these two formulations, is that the first one would have been followed by a criminal prosecution, because it's illegal, it's a national security risk to have such gross negligence. He changed it into a soft formulation so that Hillary Clinton got off the hook. So this is the first thing.

While he was doing that, he also investigated the Russiagate affair, and now it has become known that he was having an extramarital affair with another FBI agent, and they had wild email exchanges, which is now public, which clearly shows these people—both Strzok and the woman he was having an affair with— were violently anti-Trump and fanatically pro-Hillary. So, very far from being objective in their investigation, they were just acting as tools of the Obama Administration in doing all of this.

This has now come out. And it has now also been revealed that Andrew McCabe, who is the Deputy Director of the FBI, set up General Michael Flynn, the short-term National Security Advisor of President Trump. The way they did that is incredible. In the transition period, or shortly thereafter, McCabe called General Flynn, who was the National Security Advisor at that point, and just said, "We're coming over with a couple of agents." So, Flynn thought that this was a routine visit to discuss security procedures and instructions, which is normal when such a transition occurs. Then they appeared and all of a sudden it was an official interview, an official investigation—and naturally Flynn had no lawyer, and so that led to his demise.

Now it all comes out, that the FBI and the Department of Justice acted extremely improperly, to put it diplomatically, and right now there is an avalanche of articles, making exactly that point—from the *Wall Street Journal* where the entire editorial board said there has to be an investigation of Mueller because he has a conflict of interest. Then the *Boston Herald* had a similar article. There was a discussion on a talk-show about "cosmic corruption in the Department of Justice and the FBI." Others are calling for a special investigator to investigate the FBI and Department of Justice.

The tide is now turning, and there is an investigation going on in the House of Representatives and one in the Senate—by Congressman Nunes, House Intelligence Chair, and Senator Grassley, Senate Judiciary Chair. They are calling on all kinds of people to testify under oath. But nothing is yet decided, because Mueller, for his part, is also escalating. This witchhunt could boomerang. The people who are conducting the "Maidan," the coup against Trump, could become the targets of a criminal investigation themselves, and end up in jail.

So this is a turn in events. Naturally, you don't hear anything about that in the European media, and the mainstream media, but that's what's happening now, and it's even in the mainstream media in the United States. So this is very, very hot, and stay tuned with us to follow this story.

Schlanger: Just to add a couple of points, Helga. On this point that you brought up that it has *nothing* to do with Russia's alleged interference in the election— what they used to get Flynn for lying, was the transcript they had from the intercept of the phone call he had with the Russian ambassador, Sergey Kislyak. So they knew exactly what he said. Flynn wasn't prepared for the meeting with the FBI, and he said a couple things that were not true to the transcript—that's how they got him for lying. But what does that have to do with Russian meddling in the election? *Nothing*.

The reason Flynn was calling the Russian ambassador, was to reverse the hostile environment that existed between the United States and Russia under President Obama! Now, that's what Trump was elected to do, to change that. So this whole lie about "collusion" and "meddling" can be turned on its head.

Now, if they're going to do a full investigation, they should start with the report we produced: "Robert Mueller Is an Amoral Legal Assassin; He Will Do His Job If You Let Him!"

And there's one other element of the Strzok story which struck me: He was probably involved, one of the few people involved, in the Fusion GPS Steele dossier. He may have been directly in contact with Steele, and the question now being asked by Congressman Nunes and Sen. Grassley, is, was the Steele dossier the basis of

C-Span

House Intelligence Committee Chair Devin Nunes (R-Calif.), center, with Representatives Peter King and Ron DeSantis.

the FISA warrant, which allows the National Security Agency and the intelligence community to spy on the Trump campaign? This isn't getting out—it's out a little bit in the United States, as you say—but it's not getting out in Europe at all, is it?

What You Can Do

Zepp-LaRouche: No, no. And the media here are still writing about Trump as if he were a complete madman. But in the United States, the debate is shifting. For example, there was a quite useful article by a constitutional lawyer, Alan Dershowitz, who made the correct point that nothing that Trump did, or Flynn did for that matter, is a violation of the Constitution, because it is absolutely the business of the President of the United States to make policy, and that's what Trump tried to do.

So I think the interpretation of this whole thing may change completely very soon, if it changes in the United States, and the dossier which we produced is investigated in the Congress, in the Senate, and on many levels in the different states by authorities of all kinds. I can only advise our viewers again—please, get this dossier and read it. If you want to know what is really going on in the United States and why Mueller is doing what he's doing, you will find there the best documentation ever. Let me just reiterate: This is the same apparatus which went after my husband and our organization in the United States in the 1980s and in the 1990s; this is the apparatus which covered up for 9/11

and the role of the Saudis, and this is the apparatus which is now trying to mount a coup against the elected President of the United States. So this dossier is definitely a must-read for anybody who wants to find out what the "Deep State" really is. You know, there's a lot of discussion about the "Deep State," but it does not really address this from the standpoint that it is really the British empire, using its corrupt influences in the United States, which is doing all of this. So get this dossier and spread it around.

Schlanger: And in discussing the Deep State, there's the other side of the crisis, which is the ongoing collapse of the financial system. There are some new reports out in the last couple of days from relatively senior people, about the danger of this collapse. And I know you have a sense of the difference between what's happening with the New Silk Road, and on the other side, the collapse of the economies in Europe and the United States.

Zepp-LaRouche: Yes. It's very clear that all the major institutions expect a new crash to happen fairly soon. There is a financial stability report by the Bundesbank, the German central bank, which basically says it's a "Catch-22": If you raise interest rates, it will crash because there's incredible debt held by corporations, by states, and by other entities, and an increase in the interest rate will trigger a collapse; but it will also happen if you stay with the negative and zero interest rate policy—so it will happen either way.

A similar warning comes from the Bank for International Settlements (BIS), which also says the financial bubble is unsustainable. A former official of the BIS, William White, who now works for the OECD, said the same thing. There are several hedge fund managers all warning that the next crash is imminent.

We are publishing a new pamphlet in the United States, which provides the only workable solution, explaining why the United States must immediately implement the Four Laws designed by my husband, Lyndon LaRouche. These laws call for Glass-Steagall, the separation of the banks in the tradition of FDR; going back to the National Bank of Alexander Hamilton; launching a credit system; and now the United States must join with China's Belt and Road Initiative. *Only* this package as a totality will solve the problem.

In Europe, it looks even grimmer, because the European nations are in a very chaotic state. The East European and South European nations want to join with China in the Belt and Road Initiative. There is hysteria on the side the EU and largely also on the side of the German government—whatever is left of it—saying "China is splitting Europe," which is not true! The Chinese answer to that accusation was, you don't need China to split Europe, it's already split, all by itself. But there is *no* discussion in Europe about banking separation. As a matter of fact, the EU, just a couple of weeks ago, decided on new guidelines prohibiting separation of the banks. And therefore, the survival of the European nations, and these EU policies, are incompatible.

So we need to have a public discussion saying that, in Germany, for example, we have to go back to the kind of credit policy we had in the postwar period with the *Kreditanstalt für Wiederaufbau;* we need the financing of the *real* economy, and this whole casino economy has to be shut down.

I think the biggest danger right now is an uncontrolled collapse. And these warnings coming from the Bundesbank and Bank for International Settlements—they really are a warning that people should wake up and change policy before it is too late: So join us in the battle to get Glass-Steagall on the agenda in European countries as well.

Schlanger: Helga, there's one other thing I'd like to bring up in terms of the hysteria we see in the Western media. President Putin announced yesterday that he's going to run for reelection, and the news was greeted with the same kind of attacks that we saw against Xi Jinping at the 19th Party Congress in China. But one of the things that they couldn't cover up is the fact that even in Western polling, Putin is at about 80% popularity. I wonder what your thoughts are on the complete refusal of Western governments to deal with the fact that Russia has changed, and that Russia is part of this dynamic with China in the New Silk Road.

Zepp-LaRouche: I think that that is just a fact.

And the fact is that now, more and more countries are changing their strategic alignment, like Japan. I think this is one of the really important elements. There was recently a big Chinese business delegation in Japan which was addressed by Prime Minister Shinzo Abe, who announced that Japan will cooperate with the Belt and Road Initiative. So, if Japan can change, and find its self-interest in this New Paradigm, and Abe has established a very good cooperation with Putin, and if they are now working together with China, you can see that a completely new set of relations among nations is developing, putting geopolitics behind them, and putting the question of "win-win cooperation" on the agenda. As Xi Jinping always calls it, "a community for a shared future of mankind." I think this is a concept which needs to be thought through!

I made the point at the Schiller Institute conference, that we have to have a new set of relations among nations, where the one humanity is a higher concept than the many geopolitical or national differences. We have to have a notion of governance of mankind: Can we give ourselves a system of governance which allows the long-term survivability of our species? This discussion is completely lacking in the West, but it's very vibrant in Russia, in China, and in developing countries. I encourage you to engage with us, to have such a discussion: How can we govern ourselves for the benefit, the well-being of the people, where the interest of one nation is not against the interest of another nation? So let me, at the end of our discussion here, suggest to you again, that you get this report [displays the report, *Extending the New Silk Road to Southwest Asia and Africa*], because this is a study which is an in-depth proposal of how to transform Africa and the Middle East. Christmas is coming, so I think it's a beautiful gift....

Schlanger: I would just add to that, that people can go to the website, http://newparadigm.schillerinstitute.com, to see the videos from the conference that we've been discussing and that will help to deepen the appreciation of the imminent potential for this New Paradigm to come into existence.

So thank you very much, Helga, and we'll see you again next week.

Zepp-LaRouche: Next week—till then.

The Spirit of the New Silk Road Captures the World

by Mike Billington

Dec. 8—There is essentially no place on Earth today which is not touched by the spirit of China's New Silk Road process and the Belt and Road Initiative (BRI), and at least most of the world is being literally transformed. After centuries of domination of the nations of Asia, Africa and Ibero-America by colonial powers and the post-colonial western financial system, the policy of "forced backwardness" has remained dominant—keeping their economies and their populations in a relatively undeveloped state in order to exploit the raw materials and cheap labor for the advanced sector nations.

That is now changing. A new era of Mankind has been launched through President Xi Jinping's 2013 declaration of the New Silk Road Economic Belt and the 21st Century Maritime Silk Road. In his recent historic visit to China, President Donald Trump declared that the United States and China must work together to "advance peace and prosperity alongside other nations all around the world," and that the "proud spirits of the American and Chinese people will inspire our efforts to achieve a more just, secure, and peaceful world."

The United States had been kept out of this process under President Barack Obama, who instead tried to isolate and contain China's development through a military buildup in Asia and the anti-China trade pact called the Trans-Pacific Partnership (TPP), which intended to make nations choose between the United States and China. Trump has scrapped the TPP, and embraced cooperation under China's proposal for a "new type of relationship between major powers." This new relationship respects sovereignty ("America First" for America, "China First" for China, as President Trump put it), while the sovereign powers cooperate for global peace and development.

The World Land-Bridge Network—Key Links and Corridors
*Committed, underway or completed.

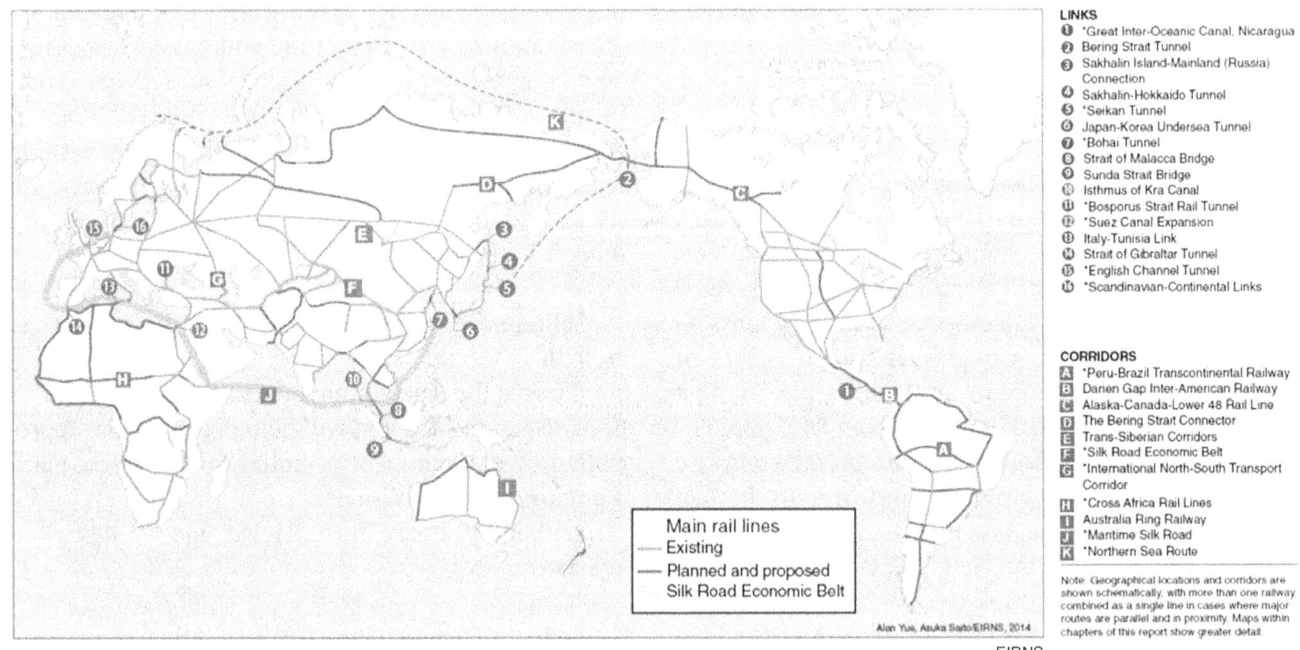

EIRNS

Addis Ababa (Ethiopia)-Djibouti Railway, built by two Chinese state-owned companies, is the first modern, electrified railway in Africa. It became operational this year.

China has performed an unprecedented feat by lifting 700 million of its citizens out of poverty in the short span of 30 years, while becoming a world leader in science, technology, industrial development and infrastructure building. The Belt and Road is aimed at taking that process to the rest of the world. While not imposing the Chinese system of government on anyone, they are sharing the method—as the Chinese say, "If you want to be rich, first build a road." Without industrialization, they insist, poor nations can never escape from backwardness, and there can be no industrialization without modern infrastructure.

This report will focus on the spurt of Belt and Road (BRI) activity around the world in the few short weeks since the 19th Communist Party Congress in Beijing from Oct. 18-24. This "snapshot" of the world under the New Silk Road over this brief period cannot fail to amaze, both in scope and in content.

Africa and Southwest Asia

A new Schiller Institute report, titled *Extending the New Silk Road to Southwest Asia and Africa: A Vision of an Economic Renaissance,* was released at a Schiller Institute conference in Germany on Nov. 25. The report contrasts the results of the "Lagos Plan of Action," an ambitious plan for developing infrastructure and industry in Africa presented in 1980, but which was never implemented, to the current burst of development across Africa, almost entirely driven by China. It notes that a June 2017 McKinsey & Company consulting report shows that China is now the No. 1 trading partner and infrastructure builder in Africa, and No. 1 in growth of foreign direct investment. Although the United States and Britain are still investing more in Africa than is China, their investment is almost entirely in equity, not in physical development, whereas in the case of China, it is the opposite.

China, like the European colonial powers in the past, needs raw materials, but unlike the colonial powers, China is paying for them—not in currencies controlled from London, but with real physical infrastructure and industries. In a financial crash driven by western financial speculation, this productive capacity remains when the bubble bursts.

For example, in the past year, China has completed the construction of two major standard-gauge rail projects in Africa, one connecting Djibouti to Addis Ababa, the capital of Ethiopia, and another connecting Mombasa to Nairobi in Kenya. In November, China began a feasibility study for constructing a 3,400 km rail line from Port Sudan on the Red Sea to Ndjamena, the capital city of Chad. This route is only the first half of what will be the first transcontinental rail line crossing Africa, by extending it through Niger and Mali, and to Dakar, Senegal, on the Atlantic Ocean.

At the end of November, Djibouti President Ismail Omar Guelleh was in China for three days, planning Chinese investment in his nation's railways, ports, a water pipeline from Ethiopia, a new international airport, and LNG pipelines, as well as concluding a bilateral free trade agreement. China completed construction of its first overseas base for the PLA Navy (PLAN) in Djibouti in August of this year, which services PLAN's anti-piracy operations in the region and humanitarian efforts in Africa.

A two-day investment forum held in Marrakesh, Morocco on Nov. 27-28, focused on the New Silk Road trade routes from Asia into both Europe and Africa, Morocco being a geographic hub for both Europe and Africa. Over 400 business executives, including 150 from China, attended the forum. Moroccan Industry Minister Moulay Hafid Ellalamy told the participants that "The Silk Road Initiative will change the map of international trade.... China needs Africa, and Africa needs China."

Moroccan Toumert Al, Education Director of the International School of the Chinese Foreign Ministry, wrote on Nov. 23 in *Global Times* that Morocco's ties to China go back at least to 1345, when the Moroccan scholar and traveler Ibn Battuta visited China, bringing back "a wealth of knowledge related to trade, governance, finance and culture." Today, writes Toumert Al, "we can play an even more crucial role within the aspirations of 21st Century China and the Belt and Road Initiative."

Speaking at a "Terminal Operators Conference Africa" in Durban, South Africa on Dec. 7, the CEO of Transnet Group, Siyabonga Gama, captured the transformation taking place in Africa under the BRI: "Africa is missing out on the current global shipping boom at the expense of its economic growth. The combination of years of under-investment and exploitation has meant that African ports, roads and railways were mainly designed and built to facilitate transportation of raw materials and resources to markets outside the continent." He emphasized that rail development was essential if African nations were to develop interactive trade relations among themselves without dependence on non-African foreign parties.

Most important in the Africa/Southwest Asia region is the urgency of rebuilding from the devastation wrought by the regime change wars waged by the British and their Bush and Obama accomplices in Southwest Asia. Bouthaina Shaaban, a senior aide to Syrian President Bashar al-Assad, had planned to attend the Schiller Institute Conference in Germany mentioned above, but was diverted by a highly productive visit to China. Shaaban met with China's Foreign Minister Wang Yi on Nov. 24, welcoming China's intention to bring the New Silk Road to Syria and the other Southwest Asian nations. "The international community should emphasize and actively support Syria's reconstruction," Wang said. "China will put forth its own effort for this." The same policy should prevail for Iraq, Libya and Yemen, all destroyed by the illegal British-Saudi-U.S. wars.

Presidents Xi Jinping of China and Juan Carlos Varela of Panama, in November 2017 in Beijing, after Panama established diplomatic relations with China.

Ibero-America Joins the New Silk Road

For years, China has been a significant investor in Ibero-America, but the pace has lagged behind its investments in Asia and Africa. That has now changed. Two major developments mark this change: Panama's transfer of its diplomatic recognition from Taipei, Taiwan to Beijing, and a highly successful meeting of the Eleventh China-Latin America-Caribbean Business Summit in Uruguay.

Panama was one of several Central American nations which never officially recognized mainland China, maintaining their diplomatic recognition of Taiwan as the representative of China. This was essentially due to Panama's near total dependence on the United States economically, even though the United States switched its diplomatic recognition to Beijing long ago. But things have changed. In June Panama made the switch to Beijing and the "One China" policy.

China has not refused to invest in those countries which do not have formal diplomatic ties with Beijing—in fact, China has offered a $4.7 billion investment to totally rebuild Haiti's capital, Port-au-Prince (destroyed in the 2010 earthquake and left to rot by the Obama Administration), even though Haiti still maintains diplomatic relations with Taiwan. But once Panama made the switch, the floodgates have opened, not only for Panama itself, but for all of Ibero-America, with Panama as a strategic logistical, transport, financial, and technological "bridge" or "platform" for Chinese investments in Belt and Road projects throughout the region. Projects by Chinese companies already underway or under discussion for Panama range from construction of a modern, deep-water container port and a giant logistics park of four and a half square miles on land around the now-expanded Panama Canal, to reactivation of the stalled Chan II hydroelectric project and Chinese financing of the construction of a cargo and passenger train from Panama to its border with Costa Rica.

In mid-November, Panamanian President Juan Carlos Varela travelled to Beijing, reporting that he and President Xi Jinping share the belief that "all efforts in public life must be oriented to the search for the welfare and development of the people." He added that Panama's strategic association with the United States is "totally compatible" with the strengthening ties with China. This is clearly a position facilitated by President Trump's embrace of U.S.-China friendship and cooperation.

Three other Ibero-American nations—Ecuador, Colombia and Costa Rica—joined Panama in a series of meetings in Beijing and Shanghai from Nov. 15-22 in order to study China's development model.

Elsewhere in the Caribbean, the Jamaican government signed an agreement with China Harbor Engineering Co. in September, 2016, for construction of a megaport by means of which it hopes to transform itself into a hub for the increased numbers of giant Chinese ships passing through the expanded Panama Canal, which reopened in June 2016.

The China-Latin American-Caribbean Business Summit in Punta del Este, Uruguay concluded on Dec. 2, with over 2,500 participants—far more than previous such forums, which began in 2007. Over 1,000 business meetings took place on the final day, resulting in the signing of agreements for development projects across the region. Opening the Summit, Uruguay's President Tabaré Vázquez described China as "the champion of international trade and a motor of global economic growth." He said that China now "occupies a central place in the affairs of Latin America and the Caribbean and a central place in the future of the region."

In Mexico, a meeting of the High Level Business Group of Mexican and Chinese business leaders on Nov. 20 in Monterey concluded that Mexico and China will cooperate in infrastructure, energy and financial services, estimating Chinese investments at $6.6 billion in energy projects. There are already nearly 200 joint projects underway in Mexico. It was noted that Mexico City was the first truly international city in the New World, when over 400 years ago, the galleon trade between Mexico City and Manila brought Chinese and other Asian goods to New Spain and Peru.

Asia Unites Behind the Silk Road

A major focus of Obama's drive for military confrontation with China was the "divide and conquer" approach to Southeast Asia. Even before Trump's election victory, Obama's intentions were smashed by the elec-

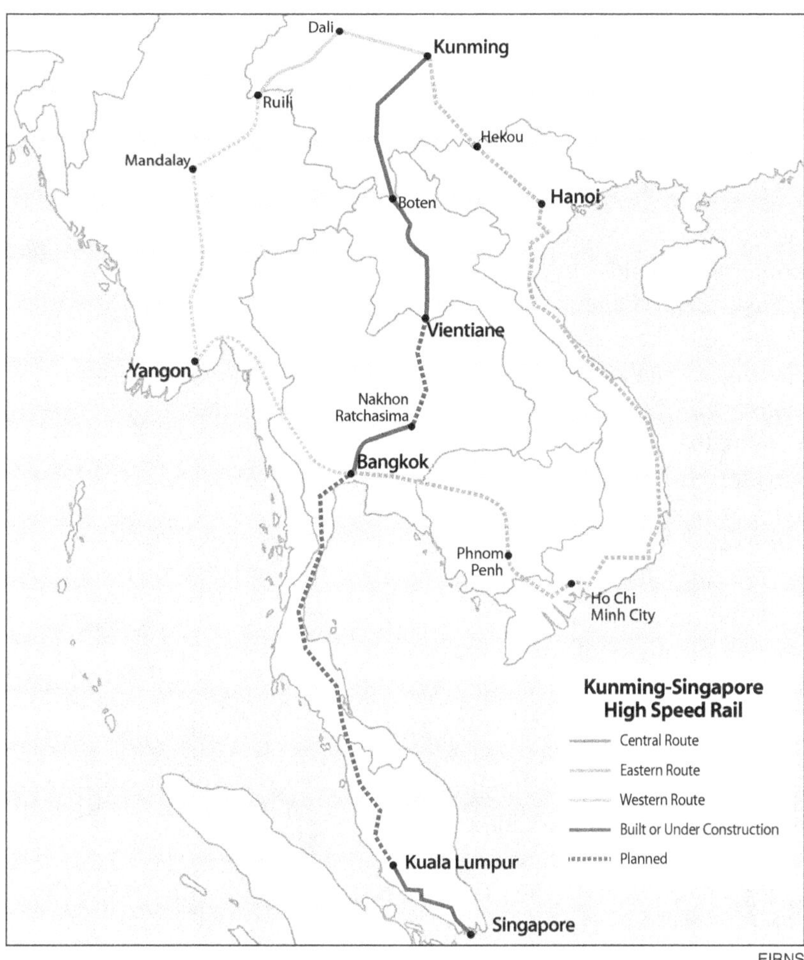

Kunming-Singapore Rail: The Chinese plan for rail connectivity throughout mainland Southeast Asia has just begun.

tion of Rodrigo Duterte as President in the Philippines, by a population tired of extreme hunger and poverty, massive drug addiction, and pressure from Washington to provoke a war with China over contested islands in the South China Sea. Duterte not only cussed out the hated Obama, but rapidly re-established close relations with China and Russia, welcoming the New Silk Road to help develop his nation's infrastructure, which was long denied by Washington.

A side effect of Duterte's election was the unification of the ten members of the Association of Southeast Asian Nations (ASEAN). The Bush and Obama policy had demanded that ASEAN members be either "with us or against us" in regard to China, but once the Philippines broke up the game, and especially when Trump became President, the ASEAN nations were free to express their delight with China's New Silk Road development assistance, while also remaining on good terms with Washington.

China's investments across Southeast Asia are massive, especially in basic infrastructure. It is building the first high-speed rail line in Indonesia, and a rail connection through land-locked Laos which will eventually connect it to the ports in Thailand. The first leg of a high-speed rail from Bangkok to Korat in Thailand's Northeast finally passed the last environmental hurdles this past week, so construction will now begin, eventually making the connection to Laos and China.

In Myanmar, China is offering a development corridor along the path of the pipeline it built to bring Mideast oil to Kunming. It will extend from Kunming, pass through Mandalay, then branch in two—south to Yangon, and southwest to the southwest port and Special Economic Zone of Kyaukpyu, which lies in Rakhine State, the site of the current crisis regarding the Ro-

Corridor from China into Myanmar is aimed at both the development of the Myanmar interior, and establishing development in Rakhine State to facilitate peace between Buddhists and Muslims.

hingya people. This is part of China's effort to resolve the crisis through a "peace through development" policy. Its three-prong plan is to implement a ceasefire (which has been achieved), agree on terms for the 600,000 Rohingya who fled to Bangladesh to return to their homes, and "a long-term solution based on poverty alleviation." This is based on China's belief that terrorism only takes root when economic depravity has stolen all hope from targeted populations.

The China-Pakistan Economic Corridor (CPEC), one of the first and the most ambitious of the New Silk Road projects, is a vast network of road, rail, power and economic zones leading from China through Pakistan to the Gwadar port in southwest Pakistan, valued at over $60 billion in development projects. There has been tension between China and India due to the fact that the corridor passes through contested territory in Pakistan-occupied Kashmir, although India had earlier permitted the building of the Karakoram Highway in the contested territory. On Nov. 17, Chinese Ambassador to India, Luo Zhaohui, told a forum at Jawaharlal Nehru University in New Delhi: "We can change the name of CPEC, create an alternative corridor through Jammu and Kashmir, Nathu La pass, or Nepal, to deal with India's concerns." Also, the fact that both Pakistan and India have now become full members of the Shanghai Cooperation Organization (SCO), which met in Sochi, Russia, on Nov. 30-Dec. 1, has provided an international forum through which to find a solution.

The China Railway Group and Papua New Guinea signed an agreement Nov. 20 to build the first national road system in the country, as well as several infrastructure projects in water management and agriculture in the Highlands, at an estimated cost of $4 billion. This will begin to address the approximately 40% of the popula-

Xinhua/Wang Ye

Prime Minister Li Keqiang of China with Prime Minister Shahid Khaqan Abbasi of Pakistan, in Sochi, Russia, Nov. 30, 2017.

tion which lives in primitive conditions, with almost no connection to the outside world.

Nepal's Project Development Committee, overseeing the country's MOU with China and the BRI, met Nov. 24. Three major projects were discussed: a cross-border railway connecting China's border with the capital Kathmandu, a transnational electricity transmission line, and an irrigation project in eastern Nepal. Other projects are also being considered. While these projects received essentially no coverage in the "Old Paradigm" media, that same media rather gleefully reported that Nepal had cancelled a dam project which had been under discussion with China, preposterously claiming that this cancellation "pulled the plug" on the Belt and Road!

Even New Zealand has taken action to join the New Silk Road. "The Next Summit" was held Nov. 27 in Auckland, with 400 academics and business leaders from New Zealand, China and other nations. New Zealand's Oceania Silk Road Network had been set up in March when Premier Li Keqiang visited, signing an MOU on BRI cooperation. Former Egyptian Prime Minister Essam Sharaf, who had participated in the introduction of *EIR*'s Arabic version of *The New Silk Road Becomes the World Land-Bridge* report at the Cairo Great Library, attended the New Zealand forum.

The most important development within Asia these past weeks, however, is the dramatic steps taken to resolve the long-festering tensions between China, South Korea, and Japan. Here again, President Trump's open embrace of China and the Silk Road has lifted a weight off Japan and South Korea, both of whom have acted swiftly to restore good relations with China.

Over 250 Japanese business leaders visited China Nov. 20, to attend an annual event sponsored by the Japanese Chamber of Commerce and Industry. This year, however, the Chamber set up a committee to report on the potential for Japanese cooperation in the BRI. Japan's Minister of Foreign Affairs, Taro Kono, praised the BRI, calling it "very beneficial to the global economy, if it is open and available to all." China's Premier Li Keqiang addressed the delegation, saying that "China and Japan should view each other's development as opportunities and contribute to the building of an East Asian economic community." Nippon Yusen Chairman Yasumi Kudo proposed that China and Japan join forces in running a Chinese-built port in Sri Lanka which has faced problems due to under-utilization thus far, saying that despite the large debt, "Nissan Yusen sees the facility as a strong opportunity in the long term." It is precisely such joint participation in development projects in third countries which is central to bringing Japan and China, and all of Asia, together.

Then, on Dec. 4, Japan Prime Minister Shinzo Abe expressed his intention to cooperate with China on the BRI. At a meeting of Chinese and Japanese business leaders in Tokyo, Abe said, "I believe Japan will be able to cooperate well with China, which has been putting forward its One Belt One Road Initiative.... Meeting robust infrastructure demand in Asia through cooperation between Japan and China will contribute greatly to the prosperity of the Asian people, in addition to the economic development of the two countries."

As to South Korea, President Moon Jae-in announced that he will be visiting China for four days during the week of Dec. 11. This will be Moon's first China visit since taking office in May, and marks the end of tense relations after Moon allowed the deployment of U.S. THAAD defensive missiles in his country, which had been arranged by the previous, disgraced government. China still objects to the THAAD, since the associated radar can be used by the United States to target China and Russia's Far East, but found an accommodation in order to restore relations. This is crucial for the effort to resolve the North Korea crisis, since, whatever the decision is reached regarding Pyongyang's nuclear weapons capacity, the only path to a long term solution and peace in the region is incorporating North Korea into the Silk Road Spirit, cooperating with China, Russia and South Korea in rail, pipeline, and other connectivity projects with its neighbors.

Europe Joins the Silk Road Spirit

Despite obstruction from the EU, several European countries have embraced the New Silk Road, and the business communities across the region have strongly advocated for cooperation. Most recently, a summit between China and the sixteen members of the Central and Eastern European Countries (CEEC), known as the "16+1", was held in Budapest, Hungary from Nov. 27-29. The Belt and Road was the centerpiece of the summit.

Over 1,000 political and business leaders attended the 16+1 summit, including all 17 heads of government, with Premier Li Keqiang representing China. The host, Hungarian Prime Minister Viktor Orban, told the summit: "If Europe shuts itself in, it loses the possibility of growth. We 16 have always been open and would always like to remain so. We always saw cooperation with China as a great opportunity." He made clear that development resources from Europe have been sorely lacking: "European resources are in themselves insufficient. For this reason we welcome the fact that as part of the new world economic order, China sees this region as one in whose progress and development it wants to be present. We see the Chinese President's One Belt One Road initiative as the new form of globalization which does not divide the world into teachers and students, but is based on common respect and common advantages."

The flagship project involving China and the 16+1 is a case in point of the difference between the new paradigm and the old paradigm. China agreed to finance and help build a new rail line between Belgrade, Serbia, and Budapest, Hungary. This connection would facilitate a major trade route for Asian goods docking in the Athens port at Piraeus, which is now owned by China's COSCO, then shipped by rail north through Macedonia into Serbia, on to Hungary, then to other parts of Europe. But the EU objected, claiming that the deal was not done through an open tender—an EU regulation—although all parties knew that no western company would have anything to do with a major rail project in Eastern

EIRNS

Belgrade to Budapest: The China offer to build the Serbia-Hungary rail connection, which is being obstructed by the EU, is critical to the Silk Road route from the Piraeus Port in Athens through the Balkans into Western Europe.

Europe in any case.

As a result, the Serbs, who are not in the EU, are proceeding with their part of the rail line, but Hungary, an EU member, is now issuing tenders in compliance with the EU regulation. As Philippine President Duterte once told his business community, which was complaining about the opening to China, "You find me as good a deal from the West, and I'll take it." No such offers from the West exist.

The "old paradigm" institutions were not pleased at the success of the 16+1 summit. Germany's anti-China Mercator Institute issued a report titled, "China's Charm Offensive in Eastern Europe Challenges EU Cohesion." It whines: "European integration seems very much at stake when Eastern European governments use their relationship with China to gain leverage over Brussels." The *Financial Times* chimed in that European diplomats "fear it could be exploited by Beijing to undermine EU rules and take advantage of growing east-west tensions in the pact itself." Of course, such tensions are the result of the ongoing economic disintegration of the EU nations under the Brussels dictatorship, not of China trying to aid those economies.

China's Ambassador to the EU, Zhang Ming, responded to this nonsense: "Some have called it 'divide and rule' tactics by China against the EU," but such concerns are "totally unfounded. China is always a supporter of European integration…. To divide Europe is not in China's interest," but rather China wants to "inject new vigor into China-EU cooperation."

Across Europe, Belt and Road forums are taking place with great optimism. On Nov. 21, the Austrian Chamber of Industry and the Foreign Trade Ministry, whose leaders toured China in early November, sponsored a forum on "How Can Austria's Economy Benefit" from the BRI. The announcement referred to the BRI as "among the most comprehensive infrastructure projects of our time." A second event on Nov. 22 was titled "Changing the Guard—On the Way to a Chinese World Order." There are press reports that the BRI is part of the discussion towards forming a new Austrian government after the recent elections.

In Italy, which is suffering a severe financial and economic crisis, three major Belt and Road forums were held in three weeks. In Milan, Italy-China Business Forum, with support from government ministries from both Italy and China, sponsored a forum Nov. 16, "Building a Concrete Roadmap for Italy's and China's Joint Growth."

In Venice, the European House-Ambrosetti Group and the China Development Institute sponsored a high level conference, "Belt and Road: Seize the Next Wave of Growth in Eurasia" Nov. 23-24, featuring Chinese and Italian business leaders, government officials, and diplomats from countries along the Silk Road.

Then, the third edition of the Rome MED-Mediterranean Dialogues took place Nov. 30-Dec. 2, a three-day forum on Belt and Road construction projects in the region, drew some 500 participants. It was sponsored by the Italian Ministry of Foreign Affairs and International Cooperation and the Italian Institute for International Political Studies. A Bank of China executive told the forum that the Mediterranean is the "key juncture of the infrastructure along the Belt and Road" in linking Europe, Asia and Africa, "by land, sea and air."

The second Tbilisi Silk Road Forum in Georgia was held on Nov. 28-29, attended by over 2,000 officials and business leaders from 60 countries, and over 500 foreign company representatives.

Xinhua/Ju Peng

Prime Minister Li Keqiang of China and Prime Minister Viktor Orban of Hungary, at the seventh meeting of China and the Central and Eastern European countries (16+1), in Budapest, Hungary, Nov. 27, 2017.

In Portugal, Chinese and Portuguese public companies signed an MOU Nov. 24 for a joint partnership to build rail and road projects in Portuguese-speaking countries in Africa—in Angola, Mozambique, Cape Verde, Sao Tome and Principe, and Guinea Bissau.

In Duisburg, Germany, which is now a major inland port for trains bringing goods from China along the Silk Road rail lines, Mayor Soeren Link told Xinhua Nov. 28 that Duisburg is now known as the "China City," with more than 100 Chinese companies in the city. "The city will be a model for Sino-German cooperation," he said.

On Nov. 30, the French Institute for International and Strategic Affairs and the Chinese Embassy in Paris sponsored a forum on the Belt and Road, with over 400 participants. Chinese and French experts in rail, agriculture, education, and culture dealt with the expanding multi-faceted relations between East and West.

Eurasia Uniting

The summit of the Shanghai Cooperation Organization (SCO) in Sochi on Nov. 30-Dec. 1, besides welcoming in India and Pakistan as full members (joining Russia, China and the Central Asian nations), focused on the impact of the BRI on the Eurasian continent. Although originally formed in 2001 to address the spread of terrorism in Central Asia, the SCO is now equally addressing economic integration of the Eurasian nations, through road, rail and communications networks across the huge landmass of Asia, Central Asia and into Europe. Its final communiqué also addressed the international financial situation: "Facing the unstable financial and raw materials markets, fluctuating foreign exchange rates and rising protectionism, the SCO members need to take coordinated actions and improve the international monetary and financial system."

The Ice Silk Road

The shipping route through the Arctic was also a major focus in these past weeks. A joint feasibility study of the Eurasian Economic Partnership Agreement with the BRI will be completed before the end of the year. Russia and China are conducting negotiations on setting up a joint venture to upgrade ports and navigation infrastructure along the Russian Arctic coast. Russia is the only country constructing nuclear-powered icebreakers at this time, and is building three nuclear icebreakers to join its fleet. Russia plans to build ice-class cargo ships in the near future.

Lastly, the United States

Finally, as a result of President Trump's historic visit to China from Nov. 8 to 10, he and President Xi Jinping have solidified an extremely close relationship, both pledging to transform not only the U.S.-China relationship, but to work together to solve problems worldwide. Trump and Xi witnesssed the signing of MOUs for an astonishing $253 billion in trade deals with various Chninese banks and companies, and for infrastructure, industrial, and agricultural investments in the United States. These agreements, and almost all aspects of Trump's Asian tour, have been totally blacked out of the western media, which instead carries numerous diatribes against Xi Jinping as a "dictator," a "new Mao" and a "new Stalin." However, in the states where these potential investments are targeted—West Virginia, Alaska, Texas and several Midwest agricultural states—there is jubilation.

If President Trump follows through with his pledge to restore "American System" policies in the United States, and follows Lyndon LaRouche's proposal to create a Hamiltonian national bank for the U.S.A., Chinese and Japanese leaders have informed *EIR* that they would be delighted to swap their massive U.S. government debt holdings for equity in such a bank, and put that credit to work rebuilding the collapsed U.S. infrastructure and industrial capacity. Bringing the New Silk Road to the U.S. is both necessary, and totally feasible, and its time has come.

The New Silk Road Becomes the World Land-Bridge

The BRICS countries have a strategy to prevent war and economic catastrophe. It's time for the rest of the world to join!

This 374-page report is a road-map to the New World Economic Order that Lyndon and Helga LaRouche have championed for over 20 years.

Includes:

Introduction by Helga Zepp-LaRouche, "The New Silk Road Leads to the Future of Mankind!"

The metrics of progress, with emphasis on the scientific principles required for survival of mankind: nuclear power and desalination; the fusion power economy; solving the water crisis.

The three keystone nations: China, the core nation of the New Silk Road; Russia's mission in North Central Eurasia and the Arctic; India prepares to take on its legacy of leadership.

Other regions: The potential contributions of Southwest, Central, and Southeast Asia, Australia, Europe, and Africa.

The report is available in PDF $35
and in hard copy $50 (softcover) $75 (hardcover)
plus shipping and handling.

Order from http://store.larouchepub.com

Financial Capitalism and the Future

This article was first published on Dec. 7, 2017, on The Dialogue of Civilizations Research Institute *website, based on a presentation by Kotegawa at the associated Rhodes Forum, Oct. 6-7, 2017.*

Donald Trump's election victory can be seen as the culmination of a series of events, including the May 2016 presidential elections in the Philippines and the UK's June 2016 Brexit referendum. These events were revolts against the expanding gap between the rich and the poor, a trend that is continuing, as also indicated by the general election results in the United Kingdom.

These events also symbolize a necessity for the global economy: the need for a transition from financial capitalism to a manufacturing economy. The reason is very simple: the financial sector widens the gap between rich and poor, whereas manufacturing closes it.

The problematic shift from manufacturing to financial capitalism began when Asian countries, including Japan, were attacked by speculators in the late 1990s. This slowed growth which had largely come from manufacturing output, supported by direct investment from foreign companies seeking cheap labor. Political stability was the prerequisite for such investment, alongside the provision of economic infrastructure. The crisis in Asian countries, which had been the powerhouse of global growth, resulted in a slowdown in the global economy.

The 1999 repeal of the Glass-Steagall Act in the United States triggered high-risk financial dealings by investment banks by enabling them to use deposits collected through their commercial banking arms. Banks began to focus on high-risk 'financial engineering' like sub-prime loans, collateralized debt obligations (CDOs), structured investment vehicles (SIVs), and derivatives.

Erroneous economic policies dictated by leading international organizations like the IMF emphasized privatization and fiscal austerity, thus reducing the pace of infrastructure building. In the cases of Argentina and Russia, this destroyed the domestic economy.

Political stability is essential to the economic growth of emerging economies. A clear contrast between economic growth under conditions of political stability and instability can be observed in the difference between Russia's economy before Putin and after Putin. The contrast between China and Russia after 1989 is also a good example.

The dominance of the United States after the fall of Soviet Union helped the rise of neo-conservatism in the United States, as well as encouraging the Blair doctrine, advocating "regime change" in emerging countries and using words like "human rights" and "democracy" as slogans, with NGOs often used as vehicles to promote the cause. Intervention in the domestic policies of other countries has caused chaos in the Middle East and North Africa and several former Soviet countries.

China never suffered such intervention, welcoming foreign factories and infrastructure-build-

The Wall Street bull.

Reintroduction of the Glass-Steagall Act is urgently required.

ing through low-interest loans from Japan in the 1990s. Domestic political stability assisted the policies enacted by Deng Xiaoping to liberalize China's economy.

Western economies, particularly their "real" economies, have not recovered from the shock of the Lehman collapse and the 2008 financial crisis. Bailing out banks without pursuing liability led to a moral hazard well-described by the phrase "privatize profits, nationalize loss, socialize risk." Despite the crisis, investment banks continued to operate various high-risk financial products. They attacked small European governments in 2010 when fiscal deficits were reported as the result of fiscal stimuli introduced in 2009. Consequently, many EU countries adopted fiscal austerity when in fact they needed fiscal stimulus.

In an today's environment where confidence in the financial system remains low, and private companies are hesitant to borrow money and invest, quantitative easing by central banks cannot stimulate the real economy. Quantitative easing creates excess liquidity, which has been used by investment banks to attack small European economies. The only sectors for which a flood of liquidity was a good thing were energy, IT, and derivatives. The huge leverage introduced by investment banks has brought about a world economy even more volatile than on the eve of the Lehman collapse.

The desperate situation of Deutsche Bank, which became a safe-haven for global derivative transactions before the crash, is the best example. The only option for a soft landing would be nationalization; otherwise, a contagion effect could drive an unprecedented scale of economic crisis, comparable to the Great Depression. In this context, the reintroduction of the Glass-Steagall Act is urgently required, in order to prevent investment banks from further large-scale risks and destroying the world economy.

In a situation of economic stagnation caused by financial crisis, the U.S. government must take the lead in stimulating the national economy because households and the corporate sector have to reduce their assets by repaying debt to banks. Fiscal stimulus, including the construction of economic infrastructure, is essential to stimulating real demand.

The Trump Effect

The emergence of Trump is highly likely to strengthen the real demand of the world economy in the following ways:

• Fiscal stimulus in the United States;

• The possibility of Europe following suit and abandoning inappropriate fiscal austerity policies;

• The end of economic sanctions against Russia;

• Collaboration between the United States and Russia, furthering peace in the Middle East.

Proposals for Global Economic Development

In short, what is economically necessary is a return to manufacturing and a return of commercial banking.

The gap between current living standards and ideal living standards exists to a greater extent in emerging economies, being relatively small or non-existent in advanced economies, but targeting a rise in ideal standards in advanced economies could be crucial for stimulating global demand.

The Twentieth Century saw the creation of numerous world-changing innovations. The Twenty-first Century has created no products comparable to inventions like the airplane. Innovations of this kind would have a significant impact on the global economy.

The Chinese Model

China can be a model of economic growth for other emerging countries in the early stages of growth when the benefits of cheap labor can be leveraged. Infrastructure-building and political stability can induce foreign companies to build factories that take advantage of this cheap labor.

Whether such foreign investment targets the domestic markets of emerging economies or export markets would depend upon the size of the domestic market. Japanese companies have invested in Thailand mainly in order to export abroad, while their investment in Indonesia mainly targets the domestic market.

Beginning as an export-oriented economy and learning much from foreign investors, China is now transitioning towards domestic consumption, thanks to its huge domestic market. This may not be possible for other countries, which require strategies appropriate to their comparative strengths and weaknesses.

Although China is not facing short-term economic risk, the long-term could be different. From an economic point of view, the largest challenge will be whether it can reform inefficient state-owned enterprises. Other challenges include a democratic transition for domestic politics. By 2025, it is expected that:

• China's marginal rate of return on investment, which is declining every year, will have reached Japan's level;

Xinhua

China's young labor force today: college students wait at the entrance for a job fair at the gymnasium of Tianjin University in Tianjin, north China.

• China's young labor force will have begun to shrink;

• Those born under the one-child policy will have become leaders in society;

• Political leaders who lived through the Cultural Revolution will have retired from the political scene.

Inequality

Several fiscal measures can reduce inequality. A progressive income tax rate and the existence of an inheritance tax are good examples. The main reason Japan is regarded as one of the most "socialist" countries is that of its progressive income tax rate and heavy inheritance tax. Many countries across Europe and South America would benefit from similar structural reforms.

A regional safety net in international financing would be a measure to protect developing countries against external risks, avoiding a repeat of the late 1990s' Asian crisis. For example, the establishment of the Chiang Mai swap agreements network among Asian countries emerged from Asian economies' tough experience in the late 1990s.

Affordable education for everybody is the basis for an equal society. Governments should ensure all children have access to primary education and that equal opportunities are applied to higher education.

Enormous West Virginia-China Energy Deal Is a 'Win-Win' Economic Paradigm for the U.S.A.

by Timothy Rush

It gives us jobs, and it gives us hope. It gives us real life. ...

I would say to all of y'all, who may be doubters, don't get on the wrong side of it, because really and truly, it's a'comin,' it's a'comin'.

—West Virginia Governor Jim Justice,
at a Charleston, W.V. press conference,
Nov. 13, 2017

The largest single component of the $250 billion in Chinese investments in the U.S.A. announced during President Trump's historic "state visit-plus" to Beijing Nov. 8-10 was a stunning $83.7 billion investment by China Energy in liquefied natural gas storage, power generation, petrochemical production, and industrial processing in the state of West Virginia. The amount, to be invested over a 20-year sequence of projects, is substantially more than the state's 2016 GDP of $73.4 billion. China Energy, a part state-owned, part-private company, is the product of the recent merger between the Shenhua Group, China's largest coal producer, and Guodian Group, its largest energy producer. The China-West Virginia deal was signed in the presence of President Trump and President Xi Jinping.

West Virginia's impoverished condition makes it one of the three states with absolute population loss (Illinois and Maine are the others), falling life expectancy, high drug use and death rates, and high unemployment. The deal is designed, on the part of both the Trump administration and the leadership of China, to demonstrate the benefits of U.S. collaboration with China's vast Belt and Road Initiative, the New Silk Road framework now involving 80 countries and trillions of dollars of investments.

The deal rests on use of West Virginia's plentiful natural gas, a problematic source of energy extracted by shale fracking. But as Governor Jim Justice emphasized in his Nov. 13 Charleston press conference, the investments are not based on extraction of natural resources, but on "moving up the value chain. ... The

governor.wv.gov

West Virginia Governor Jim Justice, announcing on Nov. 13, 2017, the $83.7 billion investment by the China Energy Investment Corporation in West Virginia.

governor.wv.gov

West Virginia Commerce Secretary Woody Thrasher, who signed the deal in Beijing, speaking at the press conference with Gov. Justice.

Presidents Trump and Xi witnessed West Virginia Secretary of Commerce Woody Thrasher and China Energy President Ling Wen sign an MOU between China Energy and the state of West Virginia, as part of the U.S.-China Business Exchange trade mission.

first thing we're going to do in every shape or fashion, is create manufacturing," he stressed. State Commerce Secretary Woody Thrasher, who signed the deal in Beijing, stated this is "the exact opposite" of U.S. companies going to China to invest in factories there, and then buy the finished goods back. "These are Chinese dollars invested through Shenhua Corp. to build bricks and mortar facilities within West Virginia that will use our raw resources, convert those raw resources into value-added finished products, which in turn are purchased back from us ... This is the best thing that could possibly happen." He estimated the investments could result in 100,000 new skilled jobs in West Virginia.

The West Virginia University (WVU) Energy Institute provides more detail and links on this initiative.

Last-Minute Drama

Governor Justice and Secretary Thrasher outlined the dramatic sequence of events just before the deal was signed, at their Nov. 13 press conference. Though there had been a 15-year collaboration between Shenhua and WVU's Energy Institute, it was a trip the Governor asked Thrasher to make to Japan and China in March of this year, under the injunction, "Go find jobs for West Virginians," which set the gears in motion. But even one week before the Nov. 9 signing, after the exchange of several delegations back and forth, the plan was close to an impasse, and the Chinese delegation had moved on to Texas. The Governor drew on a strong personal friendship with the President— what he called his "Trump card," intersecting the manifest desire of both U.S. and Chinese officials to announce major projects during the President's trip to China. In one day, the West Virginia deal was moved "to the top of the list." While Gov. Justice's dramatic announcement in August at a Trump rally in Huntington, West Virginia, that he was switching his party affiliation from Democrat to Republican, got big national press

Presidents Xi and Trump share a joke.

Senator John F. Kennedy during his May 1960 presidential campaign in West Virginia.

JFK during a campaign stop in Chesapeake, WV, April 13, 1960.

can" and "Independent" labels were not important. In answer to a question about whether some parts of the state would benefit more than others from the investments, he made clear that the whole state, and in fact the whole Mid-Atlantic region, would benefit. He estimated the deal could boost state revenue by $1 billion a year, a 20% increase from the current $4.6 billion. "That could go all over our state, education, our veterans, our disabled... it can be distributed everywhere."

The deal taps a special historical legacy of the state. West Virginia was founded in 1863 by Pres. Lincoln, in recognition of the area's stand against slavery (it had previously been part of Virginia). During the New Deal, the state benefited hugely from the road-building and other infrastructure efforts of the FDR Administration. In 1960, Kennedy famously "found his voice" in the campaign for West Virginia's May primary. His victory there was a decisive step in his rise to nomination and election. There

play-up, the $83.7 billion energy and manufacturing deal with China got almost zero national press attention. This is consistent with the media pattern of misleading or non-coverage of the Trump trip to Asia as a whole.

American System Thinking: Lincoln, FDR and JFK

Governor Justice, who built the state's largest agricultural enterprise to add to the large coal operations developed by his father, is " all in" on the deal, as he phrased it. He reflects West Virginia's identity as a producer state, in hardscrabble, mountainous conditions. He stressed elements which hark back to the "American System" of Alexander Hamilton and Henry C. Carey. In his press conference, he repeatedly emphasized that he had put labor and business interests together; that "Democrat," "Republi-

is a touching display in the lower level of the rotunda of the State Capitol (a beautiful building completed in the Great Depression), commemorating Kennedy's special involvement with the state. To this day, pictures of Lincoln, Roosevelt, and Kennedy, abound on the office walls of state legislators, Democrat and Republican alike.

In 2013 and 2014, a LaRouche PAC initiative spurred resolutions in the West Virginia state legislature calling on Congress to re-enact Franklin Roosevelt's Glass-Steagall banking law. Close to half of the 100 members of the House of Delegates, on a bipartisan basis, became co-sponsors.

The area which most galvanized Kennedy's shock at the extent of Appalachian poverty was McDow-

JFK campaigning in West Virginia, 1960.

ell County, a center of coal-production in the southern part of the state. But bad as things were then, today they are much worse. Seventy percent of the children live in a household without a working adult. The county's population has fallen from 71,000, third largest in the state, to 21,000. Life expectancy is the lowest in the United States for men and the second-lowest for women. This is the human devastation so powerfully addressed in the China-West Virginia deal.

Press Conference: West Virginia Gov. Jim Justice

The following transcript provides excerpts of remarks by West Virginia Governor Jim Justice at his Nov. 13 press conference, reporting on the West Virginia-China energy and manufacturing agreement.

Gov. Justice was accompanied by his Commerce Secretary, H. Wood Thrasher, who headed the state's largest civil engineering firm before being tapped for the position by Gov. Justice, and by Brian Anderson, director of the West Virginia University (WVU) Energy Institute and chief technical advisor of the deal for the state. Both officials made significant remarks in addition to the Governor. See the full video of the hour-long press conference.

Gov. Jim Justice: Well, sit down everybody. I'm sure you know why you're here, but there's been incredible things happening again to West Virginia. We're truly on our way. And we're doing what I truly believe is the right thing, and the right thing for our citizens. It gives us hope, it gives us jobs, it gives us real life.

When I walked in here [in Jan. 2017], it was a pretty dismal situation, to say the least. When you inherited a $500 million deficit, it really wasn't any fun. We'd drained rainy day [emergency funds]… The coal business was dismal to say the very least. What are you going to do? …We had a terrible fire in Wood County, and they didn't know what to do. The contractor that was shooting water on the fire, the county didn't have any money [to pay]. The county was on the verge of going bankrupt. Somebody had to make a decision, and I did. I made the decision that the State would back them up … The alternative was just as simple as mud. The place was burning, for cryin' out loud … We didn't just throw our hands up and say 'Well, there's nothing we can do.'

It goes back to my dad. I can remember standing in front of my dad, and saying, 'There's nothing I can do, Dad.' And all of a sudden the whole desk explodes, he grabs me around my shirt … and says, 'There's always something you can do, and you better damn well always remember that.'

At the end of the day … it doesn't matter if you're Democrat, Republican or Independent. It's high time that we all just grab the rope together as West Virginians, and run across the finish line … I'm really proud of the relationship I have, of the participation from our President. Now whether you like him or not, he's our President … He really can help West Virginia, and he's doing it right now, right in front of us…

We got a real opportunity. Just imagine this, for a second. Who in the world can even begin to describe what $83.7 billion dollars of money investments is? Well, I'll tell you what it is: 83,700 million-dollar investments. Now just think about that. For cryin' out loud, it absolutely takes your breath. I don't know if you can actually pull this off, but you may be able to rebuild every city in the State of West Virginia…

Now let me tell you this: there's always got to be somebody who's a naysayer that's out there in the wilderness and is going to throw a rock or whatever. Now, listen to me. A long time ago, my grandfather, that I loved very dearly—he was 88 years old. He wanted to go squirrel-huntin'.… I would drive and pick him up, and we'd hunt til dark and everything. Then, on the way back, we were hungry. So I stopped at Kroger's. I bought him two bags of food. I bought everything. Anything you could possibly want to eat as far as a sandwich or stuff for breakfast, sweet rolls, orange juice, and all that kind of stuff. And I put it in the back seat where he was sitting. And he started goin' through the bags. … And he looked right at me, and said, 'Could you not have bought a man a damned banana?'

Well that's exactly what I would say to you. If you can find something wrong with this, you're looking for a banana. That's all there is to this.…

I would say to all of y'all, who may be doubters, don't get on the wrong side of it, because really and truly, it's a'comin', it's a'comin'.

II. The Science of Strategy

BOSTON SCHILLER INSTITUTE MEETING

Friedrich Schiller, Confucius, and The Spirit of the New Silk Road

On Nov. 18, a gathering, which took as its theme "The Spirit of the New Silk Road," was held in Boston, Massachusetts to celebrate the 258th birthday of Friedrich Schiller, the "Poet of Freedom." The program for the event, and the many cultural offerings which were presented, were all designed to reflect on the universal genius of Confucius and Schiller, and to demonstrate the principles upon which Helga Zepp-LaRouche founded the Schiller Institute.

After the participants from many ethnic and national backgrounds heard the international greetings sent to the event, it began with a musical "Happy Birthday," a performance of maestro John Sigerson's choral arrangement of Schiller's *An die Freude*, from Beethoven's *Ninth Symphony*.

Numerous recitations from Schiller's poetry, including *Kolumbus* and the *Dignity of Women*, were presented, along with performances and readings from several of Schiller's plays, including the prologue of *The Virgin of Orleans* (which describes Johanna leaving her flock, to take the helm, to adopt the divine mission to lead her countrymen in battle to drive the foreign invader from her beloved homeland); "*Nein, eine Grenze hat Tyrannenmacht…* " (No, There's a limit to the tyrant's power); and "*Der Rütlischwur*" (the Rütli Oath) from *Wilhelm Tell*. This latter scene was followed by a reading of the U.S. Declaration of Independence.

Two representatives from the Confucius Institute at University of Massachusetts Boston, Dr. Z. Lu and Mr. M. Zhong, chose a perfect contribution for this occasion. After Schiller's poem *Sprüche des Konfuzius* was presented by Bill Ferguson, the visiting scholars from Renmin University read alternating translations in Mandarin and in English. Their participation had been

EIRNS/Jenny Burns

Christina DeVaughn singing Ernani involami, *by Verdi.*

arranged by the director of the Confucius Institute Boston, who expressed joy at President Trump's Beijing "state visit plus-plus," saying "this is the result of the hard work of the Schiller Institute."

The musical offerings were prefaced with an excerpt from a treatise on music by Confucius, on the vital necessity of music in statecraft and personal development. It could have been written by Schiller. It concludes: "Therefore, the superior man tries to create harmony in the human heart, by a rediscovery of human nature, and tries to promote music as a means to the perfection of human culture. When such music prevails, and the people's minds are led towards the right ideals and aspirations, we may see the appearance of a great nation. Character is the backbone of our human nature, and music is the flowering of character."

Soprano Christina DeVaughn, who performed at the Schiller Institute Boston's Sylvia Olden Lee Tribute in October, sang *Ernani, involami*, from Verdi's *Ernani*, accompanied by pianist Almira Izumchensky. Soprano Annicia Smith performed an original "Schumannian"

setting of the Goethe poem *Gefunden*, composed by Mrs. Izumchensky.

Helga Zepp-LaRouche's message, "Why the Schiller Institute? On the Aesthetical Education of Confucius and Schiller," was read. A recorded international greeting from Ramasimong Phillip Tsokolibane of LaRouche South Africa, delivered in his native language, Sesotho, concluded with a description of the development of a "beautiful soul," from the *Analects* of Confucius, Book II, verse 4: "The Master said, At fifteen I set my heart upon learning. At thirty, I had planted my feet firm upon the ground. At forty, I no longer suffered from perplexities. At fifty, I knew what were the biddings of Heaven. At sixty, I heard them with docile ear. At seventy, I could follow the dictates of my own heart; for what I desired no longer overstepped the boundaries of right."

Following several other performances and presentations, the event was brought to a close with a summation and review given by William Ferguson, a transcription of which is presented in full below.

The Spirit of the New Silk Road

by William Ferguson

Nov. 18—Our program today has been intended to demonstrate the principles upon which Helga Zepp-LaRouche founded the Schiller Institute:

That relations among nations must be based on the highest shared ideals of all mankind, as embodied in the greatest exemplars of each nation, each culture, for the pursuit of "the common aims of Mankind":

• That these highest ideals are based on the noblest image of Man, that each individual is born with a creative potential, in the image of the Creator of the universe, and that the most important purpose of statecraft, of government, is to develop the creative powers and the character of the citizens, to the highest level possible;

• That the indispensable means by which this is achieved is through Art—music, poetry, drama, painting, sculpture, etc., expressed in different ways by different cultures;

• That we are called to be both patriots of our respective nations, as well as world citizens, that not only

is there no contradiction between the two ideas, but that in fact it is necessary to be both, that there is nothing that is beneficial to one's particular nation that is not also a benefit to all of Mankind, and vice-versa.

These are the ideas and motivations that led Mrs. LaRouche to establish the Schiller Institute.

In the West, these are the ideas of, among others, Socrates, Plato, Moses, St. Augustine, Cusa, Kepler, Leibniz, Benjamin Franklin, Abraham Lincoln, and my friend and collaborator, Lyndon LaRouche.

In his 1988 autobiography, *The Power of Reason*, Mr. LaRouche recounts his experiences as an enlisted American soldier in India in 1945-1946, how he was approached by a group of poor, unskilled laborers ("coolies") in Calcutta, whose spokesman asked him, if the United States would export textile machinery to India, once India had gained its independence. He told them that he was only an unimportant soldier, but that he believed that America should do so. They were pleased with his response. He later emphasized that this

Lyndon LaRouche, 1988, making a national TV broadcast.

idea, that it is in the interest of the United States to promote the development of poorer nations, such as India then, became central to all of his intellectual, cultural, and political activities ever since. This life-long commitment has led to him becoming for the last five decades the leading figure globally promoting the idea of a Just New World Economic Order. This fact of his leadership is confirmed by those who have collaborated with him for this cause, and of course by those who have opposed it.

In an interview with *China Daily* a few monhs ago, Mrs. LaRouche describes how, as a young journalist in 1971, she traveled to several countries in Africa and Asia. She was shocked by the extreme poverty that she witnessed in Africa. She spent several months in China, this during the time of the Cultural Revolution. The economic conditions were poor. She describes the Chinese people that she met as "kind, but not very happy."

She said in the interview, "I came back with the absolute conviction that the world had to change, had to be improved." This drove her to seek an economic "theory to fix the problem that haunted her." This led to her joining LaRouche's movement and eventually, of course, becoming his leading collaborator.

In 1988, in a nationally televised Presidential campaign broadcast, "The Winter of Our Discontent," Mr. LaRouche forecast the reunification of Germany, and proposed that this be the beginning of an economic re-

construction of Eastern Europe. In 1989, as this began to happen, as the Berlin Wall came down, Mr. and Mrs. LaRouche saw this as a golden opportunity to create this Just World Economic Order, through the development of the Paris-Berlin-Vienna Productive Triangle, and later the Eurasian Land-Bridge, with high speed East-West railroad development corridors. But instead of implementing the LaRouches' vision of rapid economic reconstruction and development, we have had since 1989, facilitated by Mr. LaRouche's imprisonment:

- The invasion of Panama;
- IMF shock therapy, which almost completely destroyed the economies of the former Soviet Union (the average male life expectancy was reduced to 57 years in the 1990s);
- The European Union, and the end of national sovereignty in Europe;
- Iraq Wars I and II;
- Genocidal wars in Congo, Rwanda, Burundi;
- Genocide in the former Yugoslavia (In 1984 in Sarajevo, they held the Winter Olympics, celebrating sports and brotherhood—ten years later, there were concentration camps and mass executions of thousands);
- The rise of Al-Qaeda and ISIS, the Sept. 11 attacks, the Afghanistan War;
- The destruction of Libya and the near destruction of Syria.

The only nation which responded positively to the idea of the development of the Eurasian Land-Bridge, was China.

In 1996, Helga Zepp-LaRouche returned to China for the first time. She was the leading western representative at the "International Symposium on Economic Development of the Regions Along the Euro-Asia Continental Bridge," also known as "the New Silk Road." And since then, Mrs. LaRouche has become known as "the Silk Road Lady."

Since about 1989, China has:

- Proceeded to build the New Silk Road;
- Raised 700 million Chinese out of poverty;
- Recently invested $560 billion equivalent of economic infrastructure in other countries, and even paid $100 billion in taxes in those countries in order to do it. It has invested in and built rail projects, ports, power

Helga Zepp-LaRouche, 1996, in China.

plants. For example, you can watch videos about the new railway it has built in Kenya, 300 miles long from Mombasa to Nairobi, 30 modern train stations, tens of thousands of jobs for Kenyans (the last railroad was built there a hundred years ago, by the British, and it was not for the benefit of the Kenyan people);

• And China has been responsible for 35% of the world's total annual economic growth.

Contrast this to the United States, where we have:

• 90 million people unemployed;

• An opioid epidemic killing thousands, a national health emergency;

• Since the 2008 financial crisis, the 20 or so largest Western banks, the "too big to fail banks," which caused the crisis in the first place, were bailed out, and now they are 40% bigger!

• Wars, in Panama, Iraq I, Iraq II, Afghanistan, Libya, Syria.

Under Xi Jinping, China has meanwhile implemented the policies that the Schiller Institute has fought for, for over 30 years. But China did not do it because of us. Rather, the impulse has come from their own Chinese, Confucian cultural principles.

In 2013, the idea which blossomed into the Belt and Road Initiative (BRI) was first put forth by Xi in Kazakhstan, to build a "Community of a Shared Future for Mankind" based on the principles of non-conflict, non-confrontation, mutual respect, and win-win cooperation.

At the 19th Congress of the Communist Party of China, Xi stated the goal for China to eliminate poverty by the year 2020, to achieve full modernization by 2050, and to become a "moderately prosperous society." That concept of a "moderately prosperous society" is a 3,000-year-old idea that is found in the Confucian Classic of Poetry.

Xi Jinping has emphasized the idea of "the China Dream." I will now read to you an excerpt of a speech he gave in Seattle in 2015, about how he sees this:

"Ladies and gentlemen, dear friends. Since the founding of the People's Republic, especially since the beginning of reform and opening up, China has set out on an extraordinary journey. The Chinese of my generation have had some first-hand experience. Toward the end of the 1960s, when I was in my teens, I was sent from Beijing to work as a peasant in a small village, where I spent seven years. At that time, the villagers and I lived in earth caves and slept on earth beds. Life was very hard. There was no meat in our diet for months. I knew what the villagers wanted the most. Later, I became the village's party secretary and began to lead the villagers in production. One thing I wished most at the time was to make it possible for the villagers to eat meat to their heart's content. But it was very difficult for such a wish to come true in those years.

"At the spring festival earlier this year, I returned to the village. It was a different place now. I saw black top roads. Now living in houses with bricks and tiles, the villagers had Internet access. Elderly folks had basic old-age care, and all villagers had medical care coverage. Children were in school. Of course, meat was readily available. This made me keenly aware that the Chinese dream is, after all, a dream of the people. We can fulfill the Chinese dream only when we link it with our people's yearning for a better life.

"What has happened in [my village] is but a microcosm of the progress China has made through reform and opening up. In a little more than three decades, we have turned China into the world's second-largest economy, lifted 1.3 billion people from a life of chronic shortage, and brought them initial prosperity and unprecedented rights and dignity.

"This is not only a great change in the lives of the Chinese people, but also a huge step forward in human civilization, and China's major contribution to world peace and development."

China has developed and advanced, in its own way, based on its own Chinese Confucian culture. We must do that here, in our own way, based on the highest ideas of our culture, on the ideas of Friedrich Schiller, based on the ideas of the Founding Fathers, of the American Revolution. They have done it their way, we will do it our way, but we can and must do it together.

The meeting of President Trump and President Xi in Beijing last week shows the great potential for cooperation, for the United States to join the New Silk Road. All of the speeches by President Trump and President Xi have indicated that they are developing a warm cooperative and personal relationship. President Trump said that $300 billion dollars of economic deals were signed, and that soon it could be up to three times that, $1 trillion. Of course, we know that the United States needs something more like $8 trillion investment in its infrastructure, but this is a great start.

These deals include $83 billion in West Virginia for, among other projects, petrochemical power plants, which amount is expected to create 12,000 jobs there. I believe there will be investment and projects in 12 states total. And General Electric will be involved in building petrochemical energy infrastructure in other Belt and Road countries; Westinghouse will be building six nuclear power plants in China.

But more important than the practical aspects, are the cultural and personal aspects of this collaboration. The Chinese hosted Trump in an unprecedented "state visit plus." They shut down the Forbidden City and gave Trump and First Lady Melania Trump an exclusive all-day lesson in 5,000 years of Chinese culture there. They were treated to portions of three Chinese operas, in an opera house that had not been used for a hundred years. They toured a museum where ancient artifacts are being restored. And they were greeted by a bevy of Beijing school children who sang to them. The Trumps presented Xi and his wife, Peng Liyuan, with a video greeting from Trump's granddaughter Arabella Kushner, reciting and singing Chinese poetry. So there is great cause for optimism.

In closing, I would like to go back to Schiller. [Reads the poem, "Hoffnung," below.]

And this is the message from President Trump's granddaughter to Grandfather Xi. So as you can see, there is great cause for hope, for the future. Thank you!

Hoffnung

Es reden und träumen die Menschen viel
von bessern künftigen Tagen;
nach einem glücklichen, goldenen Ziel
sieht man sie rennen und jagen.
Die Welt wird alt und wird wieder jung,
doch der Mensch hofft immer Verbesserung.
Die Hoffnung führt ihn ins Leben ein,
sie umflattert den fröhlichen Knaben,
den Jüngling locket ihr Zauberschein,
sie wird mit dem Greis nicht begraben;
denn beschließt er im Grabe den müden Lauf,
noch am Grabe pflanzt er—die Hoffnung auf.
Es ist kein leerer, schmeichelnder Wahn,
erzeugt im Gehirne des Toren,
im Herzen kündet es laut sich an:
zu was Besserm sind wir geboren.
Und was die innere Stimme spricht,
das täuscht die hoffende Seele nicht.

Hope

All people discuss it and dream on end
Of better days that are coming,
After a golden and prosperous end
They are seen chasing and running;
The world grows old and grows young in turn,
Yet doth man for betterment hope eterne.
'Tis hope delivers him into life,
Round the frolicsome boy doth it flutter,
The youth is lured by its magic rife,
It won't be interred with the elder;
Though he ends in the coffin his weary lope,
Yet upon that coffin he plants—his hope.
It is no empty, fawning deceit,
Begot in the brain of a jester,
Proclaimed aloud in the heart is it:
We are born for that which is better!
And what the innermost voice conveys,
The hoping spirit ne'er that betrays.

translation by William F. Wertz,
President of the Schiller Institute, U.S.A.

Apply the Flank of the Mind Over the Next 52 Days

Will Wertz' presentation to the Manhattan Project

The following are edited excerpts from the transcript of William Wertz' presentation to the LaRouche PAC Manhattan Project Dialogue with LaRouche on Saturday, Dec. 9, 2017. Mr. Wertz' full presentation and the ensuing dialogue may be found here.

Dennis Speed: I want to welcome everybody here to today's Saturday Dialogue with LaRouche for December 9, 2017. As I think everyone in the Manhattan Project is aware, and many people around the nation are aware, we've been involved in a campaign which involves a principle which we've been calling the "double envelopment" campaign. This has involved the idea of simultaneously attacking the author of the assault on the Presidency, the attempted coup, which is the British intelligence forces deploying Robert Mueller—but at the same time emphasizing the work that the Schiller Institute's Helga Zepp-LaRouche and Lyndon La-Rouche's organization, through his Four Laws, have done with the nation of China. We have two pamphlets now in circulation—one is "Robert Mueller Is an Amoral Legal Assassin. He Will Do His Job if You Let Him," and we are about to reissue "La-Rouche's Four Laws, the Physical Economic Principles for the Recovery of the United States; America's Future on the New Silk Road."

In approximately 52 days, the President will give his State of the Union address. At that time, something has to be said to the American people with respect to the promised transformation in the American physical economic circumstance. Whether you talk about that as being a new form of infrastructure or a new economic platform, however you put it, that is not going to come into being unless our organization, the Manhattan Project, is successful in galvanizing, as we've done before, the nation as a whole, to do that.

Special Counsel Robert Mueller.

White House/Pete Souza

What we are hoping to do over the next 50 days, is create a new form of dialogue allowing the President of the United States, free from Mueller and the British empire, to cause the United States population to be brought onto the stage of history directly with Russia and China, with a new unleashing of economic power that the world has never seen. To give you an idea of how we can approach doing that, it's my honor to introduce again to everybody Will Wertz.

Will Wertz: Thank you, Dennis. What I want to do today is to give you an update on the British coup against the Presidency of the United States—because there have been major developments occurring at a rather rapid pace over the last couple of weeks, which are in large part a result of what we have done in the circulation of the pamphlet which Dennis just referred to on Robert Mueller. At the same time what I want to do is to step back and discuss the question of the principle of grand strategy as designed by Lyndon LaRouche in two cases: One, with respect to his design of the Strategic Defense Initiative, in the late 1970s and early 1980s and then, applying the same principles in respect to the current struggle which we are engaged in, and have been engaged in for decades, to bring about a New Paradigm, as Helga Zepp-La-Rouche refers to it, based upon the World Land-Bridge and LaRouche's Four Laws, including the extraterrestrial imperative of Krafft Ehricke for man to explore and to colonize not only the Solar system, but eventually the Galaxy and the Universe.

C-Span

Bruce Ohr

I. Britain-gate, not Russia-gate

To begin with, I think what we have stressed from the beginning is becoming increasingly clear to more and more people, that there was an intervention in the U.S. elections, but it wasn't Russia that carried out the intervention: It was the British empire, British intelligence. This is very well documented in the pamphlet on Robert Mueller. But there's more that has come out in recent days, which underscores this.

There are many in the Congress who tend to be opportunistic; there are those who want to make the argument that if there was Russian collusion, it wasn't with Donald Trump, it was with Hillary Clinton. But they fall into the same British trap in such opportunism. The only way you can really address what's going on right now is to focus on Christopher Steele and the role of the British in all of this—actually dating back at least to 2014, as we'll see in respect to Christopher Steele's role in Ukraine.

There is a timeline of the British intervention [see p. 43] in the U.S. 2016 election, which people can refer to. Christopher Steele was a British MI6 agent for 22 years.

Beginning in 1990, through 1993, he was assigned to Moscow, where he was essentially in the British Embassy, not as an MI6 agent ostensibly, but under a different cover. He left Moscow in 1993; he later, in 1998, was assigned to the British Embassy in Paris as First Secretary Financial. Then in 1999, he was exposed online as a British MI6 agent which made it impossible for him to carry out his functions, particularly in Russia. In 2006, he was assigned to the MI6 Russian desk in London and he continued in that position through 2009, at which point he is alleged to have left MI6 after 22 years. It's highly questionable that he disassociated himself from MI6 and the rest of British intelligence at that point.

In 2009, Steele incorporated a private business called Orbis Business and in 2010 Fusion GPS was created, headed by one Glenn Simpson, who had worked for the *Wall Street Journal*. But the interesting thing is that a 2017 book authored by Luke Harding, *Collusion*, describes how Simpson and Steele shared the same FBI contacts, and Glenn Simpson was also involved in his "journalistic" work in specializing on the Russian mafia and its relationship to the Russian state. So, they were kindred souls. The author Harding is close to Christopher Steele. Harding wrote a book called *Mafia State* in 2011, describing Putin's Russia as a mafia state.

What I want to stress here is that there is a nexus in the FBI and the Justice Department which has worked with Christopher Steele and British intelligence, including the Government Communications Head-quarters (GCHQ), throughout this entire period. For instance, it was just reported that Bruce Ohr, who was an Associate Deputy Attorney General until he was removed from that position, knew Christopher Steele in 2006 when Christopher Steele was an active MI6 agent in London. You can see in the timeline, one of the probable reasons for his contact with Christopher Steele, going back to 2006, is that he was, from 1999 through 2011, chief of the Organized Crime and Racketeering Section. Then in 2014 Ohr became Counselor for Transnational Organized Crime and International Affairs in the Criminal Division of the Justice Department. He was demoted just recently, because the House Intelligence Committee discovered that during the Presidential campaign he had met with Christopher Steele and that around Thanksgiving of 2016, he met with Glenn Simpson. These are the people who you have in the Justice Department: Ohr occupied an office about four offices away from Rod Rosenstein, who is the person carrying out the investigation of so-called Russian collusion, in the Justice Department.

We know that Christopher Steele also had very close relations with the Eurasian Organized Crime Unit of the FBI. The current deputy director of the FBI, Andrew McCabe, was a special supervisory agent, beginning in 2003, of the Eurasian Organized Crime Unit of the FBI in New York City. McCabe is suspected to be very directly involved with Steele to this day. After he allegedly left MI6, Steele, in 2010, met with members of the New York-based FBI Eurasian Organized Crime Unit in London. Basically, you have an MI6 agent who's acting as an FBI informant.

Now the interesting thing—and this is emphasized in the Mueller dossier—is that the operation against Trump starts as early as 2014, way before he even announced for office. And this is the time of the Nazi coup carried out in Ukraine against the elected President of that country. Now what has come out in this book by Luke Harding titled *Collusion,* is that from 2014 to 2016, Christopher Steele wrote more than 100 memos on Russia and Ukraine. These memos, funded by some unidentified client—and it's not clear whether this was also through Fusion GPS, which it may have been—were circulated in the U.S. State Department to Secretary of State John Kerry, and also to Victoria Nuland, who was the individual responsible for hand-

FBI

Andrew McCabe

ing out cookies and other desserts to the Maidan Nazi demonstrators in Ukraine. In 2014, you have the first FISA court-authorized surveillance of Paul Manafort—2014! So the question here is, were Steele's memos from 2014 to 2016 on Ukraine used by the FBI and the Justice Department, with the support of the State Department, to authorize surveillance of Manafort back in 2014? That's a question which now has to be asked.

Ukraine

When you talk about Ukraine, one of the things you have to realize is that MI6—which is the organization Christopher Steele is associated with—was heavily involved in supporting the Nazis in Ukraine. MI6 funded the organization headed up by Stepan Bandera in 1930s. After the war, MI6 recruited Bandera and brought him to London in 1948. Allen Dulles brought the second-in-command of Bandera's organization, Nicola Lebed, to New York City in 1948. This was part of the Nazi rat line, where they wanted to use Nazis against the Soviet Union. The coup carried out in Ukraine in 2014, with Yanukovych fleeing Kiev in February of 2014 under threat of assassination by these Maidan demonstrators—this coup was carried out by organizations like the Right Sector, which support the ideology and tradition of Stepan Bandera. So, the MI6 involvement of Christopher Steele in Ukraine is extraordinarily important. In a certain sense, this is the degeneration of relations between the U.S. and Russia—the U.S. support of this coup in Ukraine. This has to be investigated, as well as the dossier which Christopher Steele wrote, with the funding of Hillary's

Presidential campaign and the DNC and also Obama, funding through Fusion GPS which then hired Christopher Steele.

Then in April 2016, the DNC and Hillary Clinton's campaign, through Fusion GPS, hired Christopher Steele to write that dossier. The first assignment was to get intelligence on Paul Manafort, who at that point was the campaign manager for Trump. Well, this would be no problem for Christopher Steele, because he had already been involved in writing 100 memos on Ukraine previously. Of course, there are elements in Ukraine who were very much opposed to Donald Trump becoming President, and they intervened in the U.S. elections directly on behalf of Hillary and against Trump. Steele begins to write these memos in 2016.

President Barack Obama and Vice President Joe Biden meet with senior advisors in the Oval Office, July 20, 2012. From left, are: Kathryn Ruemmler, Counsel to the President, and FBI Director Robert Mueller.

Before this, you had the intervention of GCHQ from Great Britain. The reports that we have, primarily from the *Guardian*, are that in 2015, around the time that Trump announced that he was going to run for President, the *Guardian* reports, GCHQ began to pick up what they claimed were intelligence clues that associates of Trump were somehow working with Russian intelligence. And they began to hand this material over to their U.S. counterparts, the CIA and the NSA and so forth. So, even before Christopher Steele is hired to produce the dossier, GCHQ is already beginning to interfere against candidate Donald Trump, through this routine exchange of intelligence.

GCHQ Marching Orders to the CIA

After Christopher Steele wrote his first memos in June 2016, he flew to Rome to brief his FBI contact in the Eurasian Serious Crime Division of the FBI, which is the unit that Andrew McCabe was previously associated with in New York City. Then, it's reported by the *Guardian* that in the summer of 2016, Robert Hannigan, the head of GCHQ, flew to the United States to meet with Brennan to argue that Trump's associates are colluding somehow with the Russians and that GCHQ has such intelligence. Brennan, head of the CIA, prompts an investigation, by a taskforce of six intelligence agencies in the United States, of Republican Presidential candidate Donald Trump. We don't know all of the details of this, and there is undoubtedly much more that occurred. Even the timescale might not be absolutely accurate, because what we've got are merely reports from the *Guardian* in terms of these critical dates. The collusion between GCHQ, MI6, Brennan, Clapper, and Comey could have actually been occurring much earlier.

I think we can safely assume that Christopher Steele was not operating on his own in a private business venture in putting together these dossiers, but that he had an ongoing connection with GCHQ and MI6 in addition to being an FBI informant going back at least to 2010. The fact that Bruce Ohr of the Justice Department knew of him from 2006, gives you a further indication of the depth of this British infiltration of the Justice Department and the FBI, as that has come much more to the fore.

Then what happens is, in July 2016, the investigation of alleged Trump-Russian collusion begins. The person who signs the documents is Peter Strzok, who, it was just revealed, was the person who interviewed Hillary Clinton—not under oath, and there are reportedly no tape recordings of the interview. Strzok was personally involved in the decision by Comey to change the earlier language in Comey's drafts exonerating Hillary Clinton from "gross negligence" to "extremely reckless." At the same time, Strzok was the person who signed the documents that initiated the investigation of Trump—all in July, all in the same time period that you had MI6 and GCHQ intervening with U.S. intelligence agencies and individuals with whom they had a longstanding relationship, like Andrew McCabe and Bruce Ohr of the Justice Department.

In September 2016 Steele flew back to Rome to meet the FBI leadership team: it wasn't just his particular contact in the Eurasian Organized Crime Unit in Rome—this was the FBI leadership team. After that meeting is when he was told that the FBI wanted him to continue working for them, and the FBI offered to pay him $50,000. We still don't know whether he was actually paid that $50,000, or whether he was reimbursed for any of his expenses.

The British-Run Peanut Gallery

Then there is Andrew McCabe, a deeply conflicted individual. He is currently under investigation by a number of U.S. investigative authorities. One, he's under investigation for violating the Hatch Act, because he deliberately campaigned for his wife, who ran against Senator Richard Black in Virginia. She was given nearly $1 million from Terry McAuliffe, the Governor of Virginia. Hillary Clinton campaigned and did a fundraiser for her. He's under investigation for

Peter Strzok

Institute of Politics/Kristyn Ulanday

Lt. General Michael Flynn.

violation of the Hatch Act, because as a high level FBI agent, he was supporting his wife's candidacy, and she received money from the Clintons. Then, he becomes Deputy Director of the FBI and had oversight of the investigation during 2016 of Hillary Clinton—and doesn't recuse himself.

He also had animus towards Michael Flynn. There was a woman who was an FBI counter-terrorism officer, her name was, I believe, Gritz. When McCabe took over the Counter-Terrorism office in the FBI, he forced her out, and Michael Flynn came to her defense. She sued Andrew McCabe for sexual discrimination, and Flynn supported her in this effort. I'm sure the policy issue was that McCabe was supporting Obama's pro-terrorist policy on regime change, and Flynn was opposed to it, because afterwards, Flynn was fired from the Obama administration. Yet, McCabe never recused himself from that investigation either.

These are just some of the other characters involved in this. Peter Strzok was removed from his role in the Mueller Special Counsel team in August. What they did is, they stonewalled Congress and wouldn't tell the Congress that he had been removed or why he had been removed. It's now been disclosed that there are 10,000 text messages between him and his mistress, FBI lawyer Lisa Page, that the DOJ is now going through and will have to hand over to the House Intelligence Committee. But he was absolutely opposed to Trump and in favor of Hillary Clinton; that's what came out in these messages. The interesting thing is, it was withheld from public knowledge and withheld

FBI Director Christopher Wray.

Deputy Attorney General Rod Rosenstein.

from the House Intelligence Committee until one day after Flynn pleaded guilty to lying to the FBI. If that had been known beforehand, it is questionable whether Flynn would have pled guilty, because Strzok was the guy who interviewed him. The animus in this is really quite extraordinary.

The House Intelligence Committee, led by Congressman Devin Nunes, is now drawing up a contempt of Congress citation against FBI Director Christopher Wray and also against Deputy Attorney General Rod Rosenstein because of their failure to deliver material which has been subpoenaed by the Committee.

The point I want to make in all this, without going through any further details, is that you have a very close network of operatives in the Justice Department and the FBI who have already been exposed, who have a longstanding relationship with Christopher Steele of MI6, and a longstanding relationship with GCHQ. This is the intervention which has occurred. As the Mueller dossier documents, the reason for this is that they want to stop Trump from going with the One Belt, One Road policy of China; that's what they want to prevent.

So, when people talk about Deep State or other phenomena, and don't identify the British role in this; when they opportunistically keep within the geometry of being anti-Russia, they not only miss the point, but they fail to identify the enemy that's actually involved in subverting the United States of America. It's critical that that be done. And it's what we have done with the dossier on Mueller.

II. Understanding the Strategic Flank

The second point of what I want to develop here is two battles in history which Lyndon LaRouche has referred to. The battle of Cannae, which occurred in 216 BC. This involved Hannibal, the Carthaginian general, against the Roman general Varro. The second was in 1757, and it involved Frederick the Great of Prussia against an Austrian general by the name of Charles of Lorraine. The reason I'm raising these is because these two battles demonstrate the principle of the flank.

Let me begin with the battle of Cannae to give you a first idea. In this battle Hannibal had 55,000 troops, and the Romans had 79,000 troops. What Hannibal had was about 20,000 infantry in the center, and the rest of his forces on the right and left wings. Varro's Roman troops were lined up something like 36-deep, and they marched right into the center. Hannibal's forces backed up to some extent, and then the infantry on the wings basically created a V-shape which allowed them to attack the Roman forces from both sides. Then the cavalry of Hannibal deployed from the right wing and struck Varro's Roman forces from the rear. So, it was a concentric operation in which they entirely surrounded the Roman forces. The Roman forces were rendered unable to defend themselves, because if you're 36-deep, that means that all of your troops except those on the outside are incapable of fighting. This is what Hannibal took advantage of in the situation. The results of this battle were that 48,000

Romans were killed, 3,000 captured. Hannibal lost 6,000 total. With a smaller force, he was able to succeed in this battle.

Let's go to the second battle, Leuthen. The basic thing here is that Prince Charles of Lorraine, commanding the Austrian army, had something in the range of 65,000 troops; King Frederick of Prussia had only 35,000 troops. Charles of Lorraine was not ignorant; he was schooled in the battle of Cannae. He had a force in the center, and a wing on the northernmost tip which was his right wing; and he had also forces on the southernmost wing, which was his left wing. Frederick came in from the north. The Austrians had almost twice as many forces. What Frederick did was, he deployed just one cavalry unit and some infantry on the right wing of the Austrians to give them the impression that he was going to attack from there. The terrain in this area was very hilly; they call them knolls or hillocks. It was also foggy. Frederick had the rest of his army deployed under the cover of these hills and the fog. The whole army was deployed to attack the Austrian force on its weakest, southernmost wing, and up to the end the Austrians thought that the major attack was going to come from the north. So, it wasn't a double enveloping operation, it was a massing of forces attacking on one flank in this case. The issue is not some formalism of a double envelopment; the issue is the deployment of a creative principle.

Lyndon LaRouche wrote that what Frederick the Great's forces did is they "scampered"; they essentially ran under the fog and through the hills to reach the battlefield. The Austrian forces found themselves in the wrong place, and they tried to reposition, but the effect of this was that they were also about 40-100 troops deep at that position, similar to the conditions that the Romans were forced into in the battle of Cannae. What happened was, the Austrian forces were routed; they fled. And by the evening—this is all done in one day—by the evening, Frederick the Great slept at the castle at Lissa. The result here was that the

casualties and losses on the part of the Austrians were 22,000, and Frederick lost 6,300 troops to casualties.

The Creative Flank as the Key to Victory

Now Lyndon LaRouche wrote a paper called "Who Needs Brains When We Have Muscles?" I'll just read some of what he writes there, which I think is really crucial:

"The secret of military principle of the flank lies with the mind of the commander. Frederick's conduct paralleled the quality of mind shown by the scientist who discovers and validates a newly discovered universal physical principle. He outflanked Charles' forces by inventing a tactic which had not yet been introduced into the Austrian school book. Charles had learned the model of Cannae, but it was Frederick who knew the principle involved. At Leuthen, Frederick defeated the Austrians by surprising them; by doing what the Austrian commanders would not have believed were a possible course of Prussian action. In the words of the physicist, Frederick recognized a usable added dimension of the physical space-time field of action which the Austrian command failed to recognize as existing. Just so, Hannibal had recognized the folly misguiding the Roman commanders into a fatally errant tight disposition of their troops."

Frederick the Great

It's been said that Robert Mueller is very linear in his thinking. I would suggest that Robert Mueller's office is probably about 36 lawyers deep who are hostile to President Trump, favorable to Hillary Clinton, and work with the British. That's very definitely to our advantage in this situation. Lyndon LaRouche continues in this piece: "Prussian troops under Frederick the Great's command did what the Austrians had assumed to be an impossible deployment—scampering." But I highly recommend scampering when it serves a strategic purpose. "Surprise lies in the mind of him who either does not know or is self-blinded by his refusal to know, like the routed Roman commanders at Cannae."

EIRNS/Stuart Lewis

Lyndon LaRouche, at SDI conference, Washington, D.C., 1983.

What Lyndon LaRouche does in this article is then go forward to discuss how this principle was used by him to design the Strategic Defense Initiative. This was written in 1999. LaRouche devised the Strategic Defense Initiative in the late 1970s and early 1980s. He says, "The root definition of grand strategy lies in the multiply-connected character of two sets of universal principles. These are, respectively, sets of universal physical principles and also sets of universal principles of social relations; the latter typified by the greatest works of Classical artistic composition. The multiple connectedness among these two sets of universal principles defines the means by which mankind increases our species' power in and over the physical universe, and also the means of cooperation by which the physical power is developed and effectively applied."

With respect to the SDI, the physical principle was to deploy new physical principles, particularly the use of lasers, of electron beams, and so forth, to render nuclear weapons obsolete. In other words, to rely on a defense strategy to defeat the doctrine of Mutually Assured Destruction which had been put forward by people like Bertrand Russell and H.G. Wells, the doctrine which dominated the post-World War II period once the Soviet Union had developed thermonuclear weapons.

The other side of it, he explains, is that the key was to have cooperation between the United States and the Soviet Union in developing this system. The key to developing this cooperation is the spillover effects of the new physical principles in terms of the domestic economy, of not only those two countries, but of the world. "The essence of the strategy was to shift the definition of the adversary away from a conflict between nation-states, to a defense against the economic attrition which had been ruining all the leading states." So what is this, but a perspective of "win-win": a perspective of a community of principle among sovereign nation-states.

Those were the conceptions behind the formation of the SDI concept, but it applies to a definition of strategic policy as a whole.

To Win a War, Know Your Enemy

Now, if you go forward, to *Earth's Next Fifty Years* and what LaRouche lays out there—and this was written in 2004-2005—what we are experiencing today is the application of these principles expressed in Cannae and Leuthen that were critical to the development of the SDI policy. We're seeing the same approach used by Lyndon LaRouche in 2004-2005, playing out in the world, with the development of the One Belt, One Road perspective on the one hand, and our efforts to defeat the British empire's coup against the United States.

In *Earth's Next Fifty Years*, Lyndon LaRouche emphasizes that the key thing to understand in world since 1763, since the Treaty of Paris in 1763 at the end of the Seven Years' War, is that the key issue is the Anglo-Dutch liberal system. This refers to the Dutch East Indies Company and specifically to the British East India Company which took over India. He actually says in this book that the Anglo-Dutch liberal system is the "veritable elephant standing and trumpeting, unnoticed, in the middle of the honeymoon couple's bed." Later on in the same piece, he's a little bit more graphic; he says that the Anglo-Dutch liberal system is "the elephant defecating where the honeymooners are helplessly sleeping."

Now the point that LaRouche makes is that the world has to be rid of this system, the Anglo-Dutch liberal system, the liberal capitalist system, which is the system of the City of London and of Wall Street. You can't get rid of it unless you identify it, which is the problem with so many people who want to talk about "Deep State" and other such things. *That is a losers' strategy, because it's not true: You have to identify what the problem is.* What LaRouche is discussing is the Venetian financial imperial system, which, after the Renaissance, shifted to the Netherlands and to London as a center of operations, and this was consolidated in the Paris Treaty of 1763. The American Revolution was fought against this Anglo-Dutch liberal system. This has been the ongoing fight, not just between the United States and Great Britain, but between the entire world, to the extent to which it's conscious of this enemy image, and that Anglo-Dutch system, which has come to dominate.

People like Lincoln, people like Roosevelt were clear on this and fought against this, but after 1971, you had a reassertion of this Anglo-Dutch liberal system, with the takedown of FDR's Bretton Woods system and the introduction of floating exchange rates, the abandonment of the gold-backed fixed exchange rate system by Nixon, under George Shultz.

The point that LaRouche makes is that people have allowed themselves to become confused into thinking that this Anglo-Dutch liberal system, which has taken over the United States increasingly, is the U.S. system. That the U.S. is this Anglo-Dutch empire, and that's not the case. The case is that the United States has been subjected to this, as have other countries. Look at Europe today.

What LaRouche identifies as the problem is "slime mold"—i.e., accepting certain sets of ruling axiomatic assumptions. He says: "the great enemy of civilizations … is the worship of popular mediocrity in the name of a quality of respect for existing traditions," and that the problem is the "failure to carry out a needed violation" of accepted opinions or habits.

The key, as LaRouche says, is you have got to get people to realize that we're all oppressed by the Anglo-Dutch liberal system, to the extent to which it continues to exist. You have to break from that system, as the Chinese are doing. You have to bring the United States and other nations into that, and you've got to organize the world around the common destiny of all mankind, based upon the conception that the interests of humanity come first,—that is, the *Advantage of the Other*, as expressed in the Treaty of Westphalia.

As I said earlier, Lyn discusses that you need a new set of physical principles and at the same time you have to address social relations, particularly as expressed in Classical art. And what I want to do, is just read two contrasting states of mind from Friedrich Schiller. The first is a soliloquy by Wallenstein, in Schiller's Wallenstein trilogy of plays. Wallenstein was a general for the Austrians in the Thirty Years' War and he contemplated breaking from the Emperor of Austria and forging a peace agreement with the Swedes, Gustavus Adolphus. He didn't do it, but the word was out that he was thinking of doing it, and he was assassinated. The Thirty Years' War began in 1618 and was concluded with the Treaty of Westphalia in 1648. He was assassinated in 1630. His failure to act meant that that war continued to be waged throughout Europe, to the destruction of Europe for another 18 years.

Let me just read this soliloquy, because he gets at the contrast to Frederick the Great who acted voluntaristically and creatively. What Wallenstein said to himself, before he was assassinated, is the following: [as heard]

"Thou wouldst shake the tranquil, securely reigning power, which in deep-rooted sanctified possession in ancient custom, rests firmly grounded, which to the people's pious childhood faith is fastened with a thousand stubborn roots. This will not be a war of strength

with strength. That fear I not. With any foe I'll venture, whom I can see and look into the eye, who full of courage also kindles mine. It is a foe invisible whom I fear, who in the breast of man opposes me, by cowardly fear alone, to me appalling. Not what proclaims itself alive and forceful is dangerously terrible. 'Tis what's quite common, the eternal yesterday, what always was and always reappears, and tomorrow's good because today 'twas good, for out of what is common is man made, and force of habit he doth call his nurse. Woe is him who moves his worthy ancient household effects, the precious heirlooms of his forebears. The year exerts a consecrating force. What's gray from age, that is to him divine. Be in possession, and thou dweltest in the right, and sacredly the crowd will guard it for thee."

So, think of this: Instead of actually thinking about forging a peace alliance and breaking from the Emperor, which is what he had to do, what does he fear? He fears the slimemold! He fears the culture of adaptation to the imperial system on the part of the population, his own army.

Now, on the other hand, take Schiller's conception of the sublime. This is completely different. In his writing "On the Sublime":

" 'No man must must,'... The will is the species character of man, and reason itself is only the eternal rule of the same. All nature acts according to reason; his prerogative is merely, that he act according to reason with consciousness and will. All other things must; man is the being, who wills.

"Precisely for this reason is nothing so unworthy of man, as to suffer violence, for violence annuls him. Who does it to us, disputes nothing less than our humanity; who suffers it in a cowardly manner, throws away his humanity. ...

"For everything, the proverb says, there is a remedy, but not for death. But this single exception, if it actually is one in the strictest sense, would annul the whole notion of Man. By no means can he be the being, which wills, if there is even but a single case, where he absolutely must, what he does not will. ...

"To annihilate violence as a concept, however, is called nothing other, than to voluntarily subject oneself to the same. ...

"This mentality, however, which morality teaches under the concept of resignation to necessity and religion, under the concept of submission to divine counsel, demands, if it shall be a work of free choice and reflection, already a greater clarity of thinking and a

higher energy of the will, than man is characteristically accustomed to in active life...."

This is the idea of the sublime. It could also be put forward, "Thy Will be done," in respect of this concept of "divine counsel." But what he's discussing here is the combination of creative reason and will. And that is what Frederick the Great demonstrated in this particular battle. That's what Lyndon LaRouche demonstrated in the creation of the SDI. That is what is reflected in the campaign we are currently engaged in, launched by Lyndon LaRouche, many years ago, to bring about a world in which you have new physical principles — it's the Russian scientist Vernadsky's notion of the noösphere. When you create land-bridge throughout the entire planet, you are changing the biosphere into the noösphere: The human mind is redefining the entire planet on behalf of mankind. That's the new physical principle, combined with the new physical principles that are involved in space exploration, development of fusion power and so forth.

And at the same time it involves the "win-win" strategy as expressed by the Chinese of bringing nations together. It's the John Quincy Adams conception of the Monroe Doctrine, a community of interest among a family of sovereign nation-states. And the key to it, as Lyndon LaRouche says, is, you've got to get people to realize that they're all oppressed by the Anglo-Dutch liberal system, to the extent to which that continues to exist. And so you've got to break from that system, as the Chinese are doing and you've got to bring the United States and other nations into that and you've got to organize the world around the common destiny of all mankind, based upon the conception that the interests of humanity come first,—that is, the advantage of the other, as expressed in the Treaty of Westphalia; and that is coherent with the interests of one's own sovereign nation.

I'm going to conclude with that, because what I really want people to understand is the method used by Lyndon LaRouche to create grand strategy, as he did with the SDI, and as he and his wife, Helga Zepp-LaRouche, have done into the current period. I want to make it very clear that the Anglo-Dutch liberal system is the enemy, including the enemy of the English people, and of the Dutch people, just to put a point on it. Therefore, you have to see this whole coup operation against the United States, directed from the British, as an expression of this Anglo-Dutch liberal system that must be destroyed.

British Intervention Into 2016 U.S. Election

A Timeline and Key Players

Christopher Steele, Key British Operative

- April 1990 to April 1993. MI6 agent **Christopher Steele** stationed in Moscow.
- 1998. British Embassy in Paris, serving officially as First Secretary Financial.
- 1999. Outed online as MI6 agent.
- 2006. MI6 Russia desk in London.
- 2009. Left MI6 to set up Orbis (22 years in MI6).
- 2010. Fusion GPS set up by **Glenn Simpson** in 2010.
- According to Luke Harding, author of *Collusion*, Simpson specialized as a journalist on the intersection between organized crime and the Russian state.
- According to Harding, Steele and Simpson knew the same FBI agents, shared expertise on Russia, and began a professional partnership.
- Harding, the author of *Collusion,* was a correspondent for the London *Guardian* in Russia from 2007 until 2011, after which he was refused re-entry to Russia. In 2011 book *Mafia State,* he describes Russia under Putin as a mafia state.

Chronology, 2010 to Present

2010

In the summer of 2010, members of a New York-based FBI squad assigned to investigate "Eurasian Organized Crime" met Steele in London to discuss allegations of possible corruption in FIFA, the Zurich, Switzerland-based body that also organizes the World Cup tournament.

FBI agent Andrew McCabe began work as a supervisory special agent at the Eurasian Organized Crime Task Force in 2003.

2014

Steele authored more than 100 reports on Russia and Ukraine between 2014 and 2016, which were written for an unidentified private client and shared with the U.S. State Department; sent to Secretary of State John Kerry and Victoria Nuland.

The FBI obtains a FISA warrant to surveil Paul Manafort in 2014, based on his political consulting work in Ukraine. Were Steele's reports used to obtain the 2014 authorization to surveil Manafort?

Ukrainian President Yanukovych was forced to flee Kiev on Feb. 22, 2014, following a coup d'etat by followers of Ukrainian World War II Nazi collaborator Stepan Bandera. According to Stephen Dorril, author of *MI6: Inside the Covert World of Her Majesty's Secret Intelligence Service*, Bandera's organization, OUN-B, was re-formed in 1946 under the sponsorship of MI6. The organization had been receiving some support from MI6 since the 1930s. Bandera was recruited by MI6 to work in London in 1948. Bandera's second in command, Mykola Lebed, was brought to New York City in the same year by the CIA's Allen Dulles.

Flynn wrote a letter in 2014 on behalf of Supervisory Special Agent Robyn Gritz on his official Pentagon stationery. He gave a public interview in 2015 supporting Gritz and offered to testify on her behalf. His offer put him as a hostile witness in a case against McCabe, who was accused by Gritz of sexual discrimination. McCabe never recused himself from Flynn investigation.

2015

McCabe attends a meeting in March 2015 with Clinton ally Virginia Governor Terry McAuliffe, for the purpose of gaining support for his wife Jill McCabe to run for state legislature against State Senator Richard Black, a leading opponent of Obama's regime change policy and supporter of General Flynn. McCabe is now being investigated for violation of the Hatch Act.

Donald Trump announces candidacy for President on June 16, 2015.

GCHQ surveilled Trump associates beginning late 2015. The alleged intelligence was passed to the United States over the next several months.

2016

FEBRUARY Andrew McCabe in February 2016 becomes Deputy Director of FBI, gains oversight of Clinton email server investigation, despite the fact that his wife Jill McCabe received several hundreds of thousands of dollars in contributions from Clinton supporter McAuliffe. He only recuses himself on November 1, 2016 after the investigation is over.

APRIL The DNC and Clinton campaign in April 2016 hired Fusion GPS through Perkins Coie law firm and attorney Marc Elias.

Fusion GPS hired Steele at end of April 2016. His first assignment to investigate Paul Manafort.

JUNE Steele issues his first memo in June 2016; total of 16 memos June to early Nov. 2016.

Steele flew in June 2016 to Rome to brief his FBI contact in the Eurasian serious crime division, a unit previously supervised in New York City by Andrew McCabe.

Robert Hannigan, head of GCHQ flew to U.S. in the Summer of 2016 to brief John Brennan. Brennan launched interagency investigation; meanwhile the FBI had already been briefed by Steele through the FBI Eurasian serious crime division contact.

JULY July 2. FBI led by Peter Strzok interviews Hillary Clinton.

July 5. FBI Director James Comey reports there will be no charges against Hillary Clinton, language changed from earlier drafts from "grossly negligent" to "extremely recklessly," reportedly at insistence of Strzok.

July 19. Trump wins the Republican nomination for President.

July 22. WikiLeaks publishes the first DNC emails, Democrats claim Russia responsible, FBI never inspects the server.

July. Investigation opened into collusion between Trump campaign and Russia. Document signed by Peter Strzok.

SEPTEMBER Steele flew back to Rome to meet the "FBI leadership team," possibly including Peter Strzok.

According to *NY Times*, Steele heard back from his FBI contact that the agency wanted to see the material he collected right away, while offering to pay him $50,000.

Later in September, Steele held meetings with the *NY Times*, *Washington Post*, Yahoo, *New Yorker* and CNN.

FISA court authorized surveillance of Carter Page in Sept. 2016.

OCTOBER Mid-October. Steele visited New York City and met reporters again.

Late October. Steele spoke to *Mother Jones*. Article appeared Oct. 31, 2016.

NOVEMBER Nov. 8. Andrew Weismann, now the lead attorney of Robert Mueller's Special Council team, attends Hillary Clinton's election night party.

2017

JANUARY Strzok, on January 24, interviews Michael Flynn. Strzok's mistress Lisa Page, an FBI lawyer, works for Andrew McCabe. Andrew McCabe called Flynn to tell him FBI agents were coming to the White House to meet with him, without telling Flynn it was a criminal investigation interview.

FEBRUARY CNN, on February 17, reports "The FBI interviewers believed Flynn was cooperative and provided truthful answers."

MAY Comey is fired May 9.

Rosenstein appoints Mueller Special Counsel May 17.

AUGUST Mueller removes Strzok August 16, stonewalls Congressional requests for information on Strzok firing for nearly 4 months.

DECEMBER Flynn pleads guilty to lying to FBI on Dec. 1.

The *Washington Post* and *NY Times* receive a leak on Dec. 2 that Strzok removed from Special Counsel team.

Bruce G. Ohr, Associate Deputy Attorney General under Deputy Attorney General Rod Rosenstein, ousted on Dec. 7 after House Intelligence discovered he met during the 2016 campaign with Christopher Steele. He also met shortly after the election around Thanksgiving with Glenn Simpson. It is believed that Ohr and Simpson were put in contact by Steele, whose contacts with Ohr are said by senior DOJ officials to date back to 2006. According to his biography, "Mr. Ohr was an Assistant United States Attorney in the United States Attorney's Office for the Southern District of New York (1991-99), and was Chief of the Violent Gangs Unit in that office (1998-99). Mr. Ohr joined the Criminal Division in 1999 and served as Chief of the Organized Crime and Racketeering Section until 2011, when he became Counselor for Transnational Organized Crime and International Affairs in the Criminal Division, serving in that position until November 2014." Bruce Ohr's wife Nellie Ohr works for Fusion GPS throughout the 2016 campaign.

February 3, 2009

MORE ON PHYSICAL TIME

The Meaning of Physical Time

by Lyndon H. LaRouche, Jr.

My report "Nations as Dynamical" concluded with a summary outline of the economist's working definition of physical time, as opposed to clock time. Now, still responding to the same relevant question posted orally to my January 22nd website address, I focus on some essential implications of the role of physical time as such. I compare physical time, as a conception of a principle of physical space-time, with the related concept of physical space.

FOREWORD:
Leibniz on Descartes

Now, as a few words on background, I present some prefatory observations on the subject of Leibniz's exposure of the fraudulent thesis of Rene Descartes. Thereafter, this report will turn to the indispensable further development of the argument, respecting creativity as such, which was identified in the concluding portion of my "Nations As Dynamical."

To summarize the relevant leading points in "Nations as Dynamical," I state the following.

The fact that a modern concept of physical-space is distinct from such silly notions of space as those of *Euclid's Elements* and Rene Descartes, was the premise of a major step forward in modern science by Gottfried Leibniz, as in a series of his writings dating from the 1690s on. For my purpose here, let me suggest to you that the most convenient among his initial statements to

be referenced on this matter, might be his 1695 *Specimen Dynamicum.* In other writings commenting on his decision, Leibniz attributed the prompting of his own discovery of this fact to his close examination of the experimental evidence of certain systemic errors in Descartes' writings, errors which demonstrated the absurdity of the cardinal elements of Descartes' efforts to define a Sarpian (quasi-Euclidean), *a-priori* notion of the distinctions among space, time, and matter.[1]

The germ of the modern discovery of a concept of physical-time, as opposed to clock-time, was already implicit in the relevance of Leibniz's introduction of Fermat's principle of least action, and into the development of the Gottfried Leibniz-Jean Bernouilli development of the higher principle of physical least action. This initiative of Leibniz and Bernouilli, led into the exposure of the fraud of what was allegedly Isaac Newton's theory of light, as that fraud was exposed by the Ecole Polytechnique circles of François Arago and associate Augustin Fresnel. The specific, chief achievement of Fresnel, lay in his tracing out certain deeper,

---

1. Leibniz himself dated his development of this argument against Descartes from Leibniz's own encounters with Benedict (aka Baruch) Spinoza. Leibniz explained, that he had concluded that the principled flaws in Spinoza's thinking were a product of the malicious influence of Descartes. Leibniz's arguments of the 1690s were launched with emphasis on the systemic implications of some of Descartes' silly attempts at physical science. Leibniz, noting those crucial errors of presumption by Descartes, carried the further discussion of the matter into taking up the implication of such achievements of the ancient Pythagoreans which are to be considered as leading into the genius of Archytas in designing the principled demonstration of the duplication of the cube.

Triborough Bridge and Tunnel Authority

The term "creative," has a very important, specific, scientific meaning, LaRouche writes. "It refers to a quality of the individual human mind which does not exist among lower forms of life, nor a typical Wall Street figure of today." Here: the Verrazano Bridge, connecting Brooklyn and Staten Island in New York, completed in 1964.

cal," as a statement of a conclusion reached, left it to this present report to include the explicit process of discovery by means of which Kepler, among the predecessors of Fresnel, reached and proved his conclusion.

Contrary to what I emphasize in this present report, the typical sophist argues like the groom marrying what might appear to him as a beautiful bride, when she is only a wooden department-store dummy. As the years pass, he wonders (like a typical mathematician) why she never becomes pregnant! So, similarly, the sophists have argued against Kepler, and in favor of the customary, merely descriptive, reductionist nonsense on the subject. It is relevant, for understanding the achievement of Fresnel, that such opponents of Kepler ignored the fact, that Kepler's own discovery, which was a product of a conclusion rooted in a rigorous, experimental proof of principle, against which they had argued, against his conclusion, without any consideration of his proof and his development of that proof.

Dummies made of wood, plaster, or less gracious material, aside, Kepler's proof lay within his recognition that, although his experimental evidence relied upon both optical and

ontological implications of the functional difference between, on the one side, the pro-Cartesian, corpuscular notion of radiation of light which had been attributed to the authorship of Sir Isaac Newton,[2] and, opposing that, that physical principle of harmonics which had been established by Johannes Kepler's original discovery of the general astrophysical principle of gravitation in his *The Harmonies of the World*.

However, while all that I have just restated in these preceding paragraphs is true, scientifically and otherwise, what I have said within my "Nations as Dynami-

auditory assumptions, respectively, neither form of sensory conception used, could be reconciled, by itself, as if mathematically, with the other. As the famous case of Helen Keller illustrates the crucial point of evidence for Kepler's case, reality lies, in principle, outside the bounds of literal readings of sense-perceptions. As Louis Pasteur emphasized, it is what are, ostensibly, as the exceptions to the presumed rule, which are the scientifically interesting realities of life, the realities properly recognized as truly universal physical principles. That same point by Pasteur, is to be translated into practice as principles which, in and of themselves, lie outside sense-certainty, that because they correspond to Johannes Kepler's uniquely original discovery of the way in which a general principle of Solar-systemic

---

2. Laurence Hecht, "Optical Theory in the 19th Century, and the Truth about Michelson-Morley-Miller," *21st Century Science & Technology*, Vol. 11, No. 1, pp. 35-50 (Spring 1998).

gravitation lies within the irony of *the contradiction between* the mental image of vision and of harmonically ordered hearing. *The optical and auditory experiences are not the reality of the matter; they are the adumbrated shadows cast by a reality which the senses themselves do not report. The human mind, not the senses, must discover, and demonstrate the object* which these mere shadows have cast upon the sense-organs.

So, it happens, that in much of what passes for modern physical and related science, the professional does not actually have an understanding of the relevant original process of discovery, but, instead, simply relies upon the convenience of the apparently proven accuracy of some mere mathematical formulation, or its like, as a substitute for the actual process by which the discovery itself was made. The crucial issue which I emphasized in my **Nations as Dynamical**, was that the issue of the ontological character of human creativity as such, requires a more rigorous kind of consideration than what the unfortunately typical, contemporary owner of a doctorate in physical science has actually worked through. Here, we require clarification on the matter of *the ontological nature* of a principle of physical economy as such, as I do in this present report.

We must, therefore, focus attention here on the subject of the method for discovery of the physical principle of creativity in the field of the science of physical economy as such. Focus of attention on essentially relevant elements of the work of Johannes Kepler, Leibniz, Riemann, et al., as such, is (as I shall show in a third paper of this series) essential for true insight into the indispensable role of scientific creativity in "driving" a recovery of the U.S.A. and other economies from the onrushing general breakdown-crisis currently nearing the point of a general, physical-economic breakdown.

I. Effective Work Per-Second

Throw aside what would pass in **The New York Times** counterfeiting style book, or comparable locations, for today's misuse of the term "creativity." The usual meaning associated with the term "creative," is, scientifically, mumbling nonsense; often, the defense of such nonsense as the **Times**', is of the form, "None of the friends I trust will disagree with me." Contrary to such pathetic expressions of opinion as that, in competent scientific practice, "creative" has a specific, and rarely recognized, special meaning, a meaning which

does not exist in the lexicons of typical, recent university graduates, or relevant others, today.

Properly employed, that term, "creative," does have a very important, specific, scientific meaning. It refers to *a quality of the individual human mind which does not exist among lower forms of life, nor a typical Wall Street figure of today.* It refers to a term whose true meaning is rarely intended when the term "creativity" is ordinarily employed in academic, or related usage today.

To identify a much-needed, competent definition for the term "creativity," we must restrict the term's use, either to principles of nature which exist, and which in forms of life lower than mankind, but, even among our species, rarely occur as an expression of voluntary willfulness today, except among exceptional members of our human species, and that, so far.

Nonetheless, the proper use of the term is definitely limited, in the sense that it can be identified in a rigorous way, but that is only in a way which lends itself to the actual idea of creation, the quality of being susceptible of communication, even to persons who had been ignorant of even the very existence, and efficiency, of such an actual idea as I have defined it.

That said, take a case with which some among my younger scientific associates have become familiar, and that, happily, with increasing competence. Take the exemplary case on which all competent modern science is premised by reference, the case of Johannes Kepler's creative action in his uniquely original discovery of the general principle of the system of Solar orbits, as in his **The Harmonies of the World**.[3] The work by Kepler (with emphasis on **Harmonies**) is, for special reasons which I shall indicate in this present report, the proper beginning of an economically competent general practice of modern physical science; therefore, it provides us a standard of reference for the meaning of the notion of a specifically creative act of discovery within the bounds of the category of modern science as such.

That is an example of what I mean by true creativity.

The principal source of widespread difficulty respecting even the mere definition of "scientific discovery," has usually been, historically, a prevalent pattern in the known societies of ancient through modern history, a pattern typified, symptomatically, by the central

---

3. Admittedly, the title of Kepler's work is often mistranslated as **The Harmony of the World**, rather than the proper **The Harmonies** (or, "harmonics") **of the World**.

issue of Aeschylus' ***Prometheus Bound***.

Before turning attention, directly, to what I have just referenced as the function of human creativity as such, it is essential that we first focus on the socially systemic, academic, or other obstacles to recognizing the functioning of the human potential for creativity.

The Obstacle to Reason

The significance of Aeschylus' ***Prometheus Bound***, is located in its thematic issue. That is, the Olympian Zeus' ban on human creativity: which shows Zeus's intended bestialization of all mortal human individuals, by forbidding, not only the use, but the discovery of any universal physical principle, such as "fire," or, today, nuclear-fission power. That issue arises in the location of this present writing by me, as the way in which human beings are actually conditioned, at least usually so, as in the contemporary U.S.A. and Europe, against any actually intentional employment of their individual creative powers, those creative powers which distinguish human beings from all lower forms of life. Thus, the very idea of the existence of an actual phenomenon of creation does not exist in the mind of the usual certified financial accountant, nor in the mind of most of today's faculty members of leading academic science departments or economics faculties.

Every gifted child has experienced the effect of that "Olympian law" of Zeus. Thus, any young person, as in schools, who shows the activation of his, or her actually creative mental powers, will probably become the "black chick" targeted for pecking by the "white chicks," as if he, or she were a virtual "outsider," if not actually comparable to an African-American at a Klan rally. Thus, it is usual to see that youth of the so-called "higher IQ" categories often seek to avoid hostile pecking by the "white chicks," by withdrawing from behavior which tends to bring them into that kind of attack which is set off when signs of their own more developed mental potential enrage the "white chicks," as the presence of the legendary swan enrages the ducks. If the more gifted student, for example, behaves naturally, generally, that student is often made "fair game" for

As late as the early 1950s, LaRouche reports, he was the target of anti-Semitic attacks, prompted by the fact that his heavy-rimmed spectacles marked him as one of those "brainy Jews," among certain "anti-intellectuals." Shown, LaRouche at a meeting in 1973, in New York.

mob-like attacks by some among the "white chicks." Even teachers in public schools and professors in universities have often tended to ally themselves, as more or less open sponsors, with the relevant "white chicks'" mob-like behavior.

Why did the "white chicks" (and many among today's relevant types of faculty members) tend to behave in such a brutish fashion?

For example, in my personal observation, during the 1930s and later, "anti-semitism" of the 1945 "VE-Day" American populists over the interval from about the 1920s through 1940s, was associated with hatred of the child or adolescent, for example, who was suspected of being among "those brainy Jews." (Sometimes persons stereotyped as an "outsider" to "our American populist way of life" as in the mind of some American or European as being of Asian or African, or Spanish-American origins might be treated similarly.) The typical "free trade" fanatic of politics still today, especially that of Yahoo-like, populist leaning toward racist hatreds, tends to fit the category of the "populist" anti-intellectual depravity mustered in support of the wildest, pill-taking and other radio and TV fanatics of that sort.[4]

---

4. For example, as late as the early 1950s, I was still the target of anti-Semitic attacks which were prompted by the fact that my heavy-rimmed spectacles marked me as "obviously Jewish" among the typical representative of the "anti-intellectual" classes.

On the opposite side, that love for other people which we should associate with the "Westphalia Principle," is a reflection of the high regard a civilized human individual feels for all other sections of mankind, a love for that creative potential which distinguishes men and women from feral beasts, or beast-like populist fanatics, including the typical, ego-ridden, dumb religious fanatic.

Why should those "white chick" sets behave with such frequent hostility toward those portions of their own society and age-groups which would tend to make the relatively greatest contribution to the benefit of them all?

The result of those referenced, historically prevalent, "conditioned" forms of obstacles to actually creative thinking, which are often encountered among the majority of today's populations, has been the predominant characteristic of virtually all known human cultures. Think of that majority as like the Prometheus-haters among the Olympian lackeys of the Zeus as portrayed by Aeschylus' ***Prometheus Bound***.

How and why such prevalent habits of known cultures differ from one another, and, more important, why they tend to converge in certain common features of their malicious effects, begs a broader study of those histories than is needed for our purposes in this present report. A few typical cases are sufficient, as matters of background, to provide a setting in which the specific purpose of this present report can be realized. That done, we will have now made my foregoing point clear enough for our purposes in this present report.

Take the case of the a-priori assertions of alleged principle which circumscribe the contents of a Euclidean geometry; treat this effect of Euclidean brainwashing as a key illustration of a general form of the method which has been employed, in classrooms and elsewhere, to prevent individuals from employing their innate, human creative potentials. In this regard, the opening two paragraphs, and concluding sentence of Bernhard Riemann's 1854 habilitation dissertation, when juxtaposed, provide us with the model form of something likely to incite a direct attack of resentment, an attack intended to suppress "the ferment of human individual creativity" within the population, a brutish attack made in the fascist-like effort to terrorize the target into a state of cultural submission to the populist mediocrities of the many.

Thus, in that observation, we have the background, to recognize the essential characteristics of the sundry, ignorance-fed expressions of those forms of mass suppression of scientific-technological progress, such as malthusianism, or today's neo-malthusian ("green") mass-stupefaction of populations, as by the World Wildlife Fund of the current Duke of Edinburgh; his son, the Prince of Wales; the late Prince Bernhard of the Netherlands; and Philip's American puppet, the perverse former U.S. Vice-President Al Gore, complementing forms of brainwashing such as Euclidean geometry.

Sarpi's Liberal Syndrome

Take that case of Britain's Duke of Edinburgh, as a typical expression of the evil embodied in the modern Anglo-Dutch Liberalism which was launched, in the aftermath of the famous Sixteenth-Century Council of Trent, launched by the initiative of the systemic irrationalist, and anti-Trent fanatic, Paolo Sarpi.

Whereas, Sarpi's rivals, the Aristoteleans, imposed a simple suppression of knowledge of the existence of human creativity, Sarpi substituted a systemic irrationalism modeled, by his own choice, upon that of that wildly immoral, medieval irrationalist William of Ockham. The practical significance of the difference is that, whereas, the clerical Aristoteleans insisted upon the suppression of creativity in society, Sarpi allowed technological and related forms of innovation, insofar as this license did not permit the consideration of a discovery of actual universal physical principles. This ideological strategy by Sarpi permitted the faction of Venetian usury oriented to the northern maritime regions of Europe, to choose a prospect of relatively greater military and other power, at the expense, strategically, of those relatively more backward devotees of Aristotle.[5]

Whereas, as Friedrich Schiller presented the image of religious warfare, in the Netherlands, and also, in his ***Wallenstein*** Trilogy, the clerical adherents of the nominally Aristotelean dogma, were no less irrational in their part as practitioners of post-1492, Nazi-like religiously motivated mass-homicide, than Sarpi's nominally Protestant followers of a revived cult of the medieval irrationalist William of Ockham. As the leading figure of the Eighteenth Century British Empire, Lord Shelburne, understood, the British Empire whose strategy for empire was based on a commitment to the heri-

---

5. The superiority of the Anglo-Dutch Liberals over the others, was concentrated in superiority of Anglo-Dutch Liberal and related forms of maritime superiority over the Mediterranean region, as the latter is typified by the Eighteenth-century ruin of the silly Spanish Armada.

From the time of the Napoleonic wars, which ruined continental Europe to British advantage, the policy of the Liberal followers of Paolo Sarpi et al., has been to destroy scientific and cultural progress. Shown, Francisco Goya's treatment of the Napoleonic wars in Spain, in his "Disasters of War" (c. 1820); this etching is titled, "With or Without Reason."

tage of Julian the Apostate, all European empires, ancient through modern have premised the maintenance of their power on the emperor's reign by the power of the pantheon, as they did by playing one religious sect in virtual, or actual perpetual warfare against another.

The carnage of the pre-Westphalia conflict between the Protestant and Catholic religious party, from 1492 through 1648, was nothing other than two sets of the common dupes held in bondage to mutual slaughter, as in the case of the Sykes-Picot-ridden Middle East still today.

So, through the advantage represented by Sarpi's criminal-minded, Liberals' evasion of the strategically self-crippling characteristics of medieval and modern Aristotelean brutishness, Sarpi founded what was to become a new Venetian world empire, called, now, conventionally, a British, or Anglo-Dutch, or the post-1971-73, Anglo-Dutch-Saudi world empire of international financier rule through manipulation of the dupes into the game of religious or kindred perpetual, regular or irregular warfare. This British empire, which, since 1968-1973, has functioned as the only actual empire in the world today by acting through a policy of suppressing investment in relevant forms of scientific and tech-

nological progress, including the suppression of the development of productive investments in basic economic infrastructure. The true religion of the British monarchy and its principal subjects, is not the worship of God, but of the god of usury defined, in principle, by Adam Smith in Smith's 1759 ***Theory of the Moral Sentiments***.

So, the same movement of Sarpi which employed Liberal approaches to the use of merely technological, rather than actually scientific progress, to gain a strategic advantage of its Habsburg-linked rivals, reacted, itself, against the surge of the actual science which had been launched by Kepler's revolutionary discoveries. They reacted so against France's Cardinal Mazarin and Jean-Baptiste Colbert, and against Gottfried Leibniz, above all others. From the time of the Napoleonic wars of that foolish Napoleon Bonaparte who ruined continental Europe to British advantage with his wars, the policy of the Liberal followers of Sarpi et al., has been, to the present date, to destroy the kind of scientific and cultural progress which can be achieved only through its realization in the increase of the productive powers and cultural development of the general population.

So, Napoleon Bonaparte lies like a hero's corpse in Paris. Either he was consciously a British agent, in his role of conducting what was, in fact, a new "Seven Years War" on London's behalf, or, he did the job of securing a semi-permanent tyranny, by London and Amsterdam over continental Europe without knowing what a manipulated fool he was.[6]

Thus, the triumph of Britain (e.g., the Anglo-Dutch-

---

6. The entirety of British imperial policy, from the 1890 ouster of Germany's Bismarck from the post of Chancellor, and including the assassination of France's President Sadi Carnot, the British 1894 launching of a continuing pattern of Japan's warfare against China during the 1895-1945 interval, the assassination of U.S. President McKinley, the 1905 warfare, World War I, World War II, and the so-called "Cold War," have been, each and all, an extension of the strategy of the so-called "Seven Years War" which first established Lord Shelburne's British East India Company as a private empire with a private army and navy of its own.

Saudi new Venetian empire) over the U.S.A. and continental Europe since 1968-1973, is the sole principal cause of the presently ongoing general breakdown-crisis form of global economic collapse of the entire planet now.[7]

The principal characteristic of this general, global economic collapse of the planet has been the "new malthusianism" imposed by the influence of both the British empire and the "environmentalist" swindle of British dupes such as the wildly lying, former U.S. Vice-President Al Gore. Solar panels and windmills are the hallmarks of the advent of the world now into the already quivering brink of a planetary form of new dark age far, far worse than that which struck Europe during the notorious Fourteenth-Century "New Dark Age."

Science versus Liberalism

To the best of my knowledge, and my knowledge is, on its record of performance since 1956-57, manifestly far superior relative to any other so-called "authority" in the field of economics throughout the world today, there has been, presently no competence in long-range economic forecasting among my rivals among nominally professional, putative economics and related professionals in the world today.

Earlier, during the 1950s and early 1960s, our relative successes in national economies in the U.S.A., some other parts of the Americas, in western and central continental Europe, Australia, and in the Asian rim of the Pacific were not due to any particular competence in the practice of economic theory, but, rather, were chiefly products of reliance on scientific and technological progress in increase of the physical-productive powers of labor, as in agriculture, the machine-tool-design side of industrial practice, and in programs in infrastructure such as those launched by President Charles de Gaulle's

Fifth Republic. The financier community's role has been, chiefly a parasite, and the economists were chiefly, usually, at their moral best, a nuisance; but, certain habits of national agro-industrial and infrastructural progress had been embedded in the aftermath of the experiences of World War II. Although that happier impulse was already waning even before the assassination of President John F. Kennedy, its waning impact had been still strong.

By the end of the 1970s, the impact of the World War II generation was already waning; as the 68ers' influence took over, more and more, the forces which had fought World War II and its aftermath, were leaving the site. With the disgusting developments of the 1968-1973 interval, the pathetic strains of the ideology of the "68ers" were now the reigning trend. The fatal economic downturn then reigning inside North America and Europe (most notably) will now continue, to its early catastrophic end, unless a new cultural impact conveyed by the relative best among an emerging young-adult generation now in their twenties and thirties, exerts the degree of relative influence at the top which the 68ers found during the 1970s and 1980s, a generation or more ago.

The point I am stressing at this point, is that there is an important, sometimes crucial distinction to be made, between acquired habits of one generation, and the direction of change represented by an oncoming younger one. The impact of my own family tradition in these United States, which is traced in my genealogy since the Mayflower and Massachusetts Bay colony, has helped greatly in teaching me to think of policy-shaping over a span of centuries, not a mere few years, even a decade. In general, no individual has much of a mark on his culture's history during a lapsed span of less than a generation, a generation being the span of a cycle of capital investment in production, and a much longer span, of two generations span, or more, that of investment in the types of basic economic infrastructure.

The nations of the U.S.A. and western and central Europe today, are fairly regarded as presently under the control of most extremely neurotic knee-jerk cultures. That is to point to what has become the generational span of those changes in economic and related policy of practice which are associated with revolutionary surges of scientific progress.

It is, perhaps, fortunate for us, that the new U.S. President is almost two generations younger than I am; thus, if he is permitted to do his job, and actually does it

---

7. The collapse of the U.S. dollar had been caused by the British floating of the pound sterling in Autumn 1967. However, already, during the middle to late 1950s, I had foreseen the threat of a decades-long decline of the U.S. economy. Until the middle of the 1960s, I consider that decline to be an active, probable threat. By 1967-68, I was assured that a long-term general breakdown-crisis was already in progress in the trans-Atlantic economies. As I announced in my July 25, 2007 webcast, I announced that what is now clearly the presently onrushing general breakdown-crisis of the existing world monetary system, is absolutely certain. Only the installation of a new credit-system, to replace the present monetary system, could save global civilization from a presently onrushing new dark age; without a U.S. leading initiative in launching a new credit-system, to replace the useless monetary systems, there is no happy change for mankind in the generations immediately ahead.

decently, he has a prospective life-span long enough to come to amount to something useful for our society, and the world.

II. Science, Money & Economy

That much said in the preceding pages of this present report, so far: the essential point to be considered here, is the fact that human beings, unlike any other living species, have the inborn power to make actually creative discoveries of principle which, once adopted by society, change the universe, at least implicitly so. *Man is not merely an inhabitant of this universe, but is made in the actual likeness of the universe's Creator.* That is not an opinion, but a scientific fact.

Other species, including all the different orders of living species other than mankind, lack what is uniquely a quality specific to mankind; but, humanity expresses a universal, determining, characteristic principle which itself is lacking in the ecology specific to each of all known orders of life apart from mankind. It is the principle of mankind, which distinguishes mankind from the beasts.

At this point of the report, my attention, and, implicitly yours, is focused on a more modest aspect of the aforesaid general principle. My attention is focused upon that principle of human life which underlies any competent conception of a real economic principle for guiding human society's existence and progress.

The existence of the human population is conditional upon society's currently relevant *potential relative population-density.* Unlike all other living species and their varieties, the human race is the only living species which does not share the characteristics of population of sets (systems) of animal ecological systems. Mankind's equivalent of an ecological population-potential is variable. This variability is chiefly located in the increase of the capability of the human species through its intellectual development. This fact is most boldly underlined by a simple contrast of the increase of the human population of the planet relative to the level of the higher apes.

Thus, the success or failure of human ecologies depends chiefly on the factor of scientific progress, as that progress is embedded in influence and effect through increase of the physical productive powers of labor, as this occurs through realization of discoveries of fundamental scientific principles which are expressed as up-ward-directed changes in the culture of societies as a whole, or, on the contrary, in the relative cultural stagnation, stagnation of practices by component portions, more or less "neo-Malthusian" rabble among that culture's population.

In the end, it is the discovery and application of what is called fundamental scientific and cultural progress, which predetermines the rise and fall of cultures. Thus, a policy and practice of cultural zero-growth policy of any society, as in the U.S.A. under the growing influence of the pro-Malthusian "68ers" during the recent four decades, dooms that culture by its own hand. That is to emphasize that man's ability to sustain even a fixed level of population demands sufficient progress to offset the inevitable effects of attrition. The success of the human species, its fundamental superiority as a living species over all animal species, "condemns" it to a commitment to what is, ultimately, fundamental scientific progress in the practice of physical economy, per capita and per square kilometer of territory.

These matters of discoveries have the quality of universal physical principles, as typified by that principle of universal gravitation discovered, uniquely, by Johannes Kepler. They are, to speak of this matter here in terms of relative modesty, ideas respecting economy which have the same quality of power in the universe as the uniquely original discovery of the principle of universal gravitation by Johannes Kepler. No other living species has shown mankind's manifest ability to do this.

That means, that to survive, today's civilization must be, immediately, now, suddenly, and radically changed, back to policies consistent with the trends expressed by President Franklin Roosevelt. Otherwise, the so-called "environmentalist" trends of the recent forty-odd years have already certainly doomed this planet as a whole to an immediate plunge into a new dark age, in which population-levels might bottom out at about one billion individuals, or less. Either those trends are now suddenly, and profoundly changed in favor of what I have preferred, or there is no hope for civilization during several generations to come,—and, as I have been repeatedly shown, over about five decades, to have been the best long-range economic forecaster alive.[8]

So, human creativity, as I have just summarily de-

---

8. I may not be perfect, but I am the only known forecaster, world wide, employing a competent method.

EIRNS/James Rea

Unless "environmentalist" trends are immediately reversed, this planet were certainly doomed to an immediate plunge into a new dark age, in which the human population might bottom out at about 1 billion individuals, or fewer. Shown: an anti-nuclear demonstration in Berlin, Germany. The sign says, "Nuclear waste disposal now in your backyard."

scribed it, is a specific quality of the human mental, willful potential, a quality which does not appear in any other living species, and *has no root in the biological apparatus of any other living species*. This means, as I shall present this case during the course of the remainder of this present report, and that successor soon to follow, that: in the expression of actual human creativity, such as Kepler's uniquely original discovery of universal gravitation, the human mind "taps into" a power within the universe, a power which is not to be found as rooted within the bounds of the capabilities of all other living species.

It is this latter distinction of mankind, to which we allude, when we speak of mankind as having a power, that of a soul, a power which is not a by-product of biological creatures as we know them otherwise, but which equips human beings and their societies with a genuinely creative potential, if we choose to accept that gift to us.

This potential is therefore associated with something specific to the manifestations of the human brain-function in some way, as a power which is clearly associated with the human brain's expressed function, but a power which does not exist in the brain of any other living species. The evidence is, that something in the nature of the human species has developed the ability to "tune into," as if by a mode of coupling, some higher power in the universe, as no other known species has done. It can be restated: that the specific distinction of the manifest creative powers of the human mind, is that it is susceptible of being tuned into the principle of the Creator of the universe. In other words, that power can not be a by-product of biology as customarily defined by science so far, but is, as I shall address this in the forthcoming, concluding part of this series of reports, rather, "tuned into," *dynamically*, a power which is of a specifically higher quality than the evolutionary potential of living processes otherwise.

The Dynamics of Economy

What I have just said on this account, is not speculation; it is a practical fact defined by the specific, manifest, practical, experimentally accessible distinction of the human species from all others. Such is the creative genius expressed by such as Riemann, Einstein, and Vernadsky.

When I refer, as I do here, to "tapping into" some power which is not identifiable as contained within the individual member of society (or any other comparably relevant kind of process), we are in the domain of *dynamics*, as Leibniz employed that conception. The actual expression of what we should intend to mean when we employ the term "dynamics" in physical science, is that in addition to discrete objects of sense-perception, or related kinds of matters, the form of organization within whose bounds such local manifestations exist, is itself an efficient object of scientific conception.

This distinction arises inevitably when we are impelled to reflect upon the fact that space and time as defined by Euclid, or Descartes, do not actually exist; but, rather that space and time are expressions of objects of a special kind, which act upon, and are acted upon by what we otherwise recognize as akin to our intention in pointing toward discrete objects. Call them *"indiscrete* objects," (sic) forms of dynamics which are themselves a special quality of physically efficient kind of conceptual object, as Leibniz defined modern dynamics, since they tend to meddle everywhere, as universal gravitation does, when that interference were liked, or not.

What I have just said in the preceding paragraphs, had begun to become clear to science's experience in the aftermath of that line of qualitative development of modern science, through such developments as the skein of those discoveries of principle leading from the work of Nicholas of Cusa, Leonardo da Vinci, and Johannes Kepler. However, the point I am making here and now, could not have been made explicitly, until the way had been cleared for this, as it was for me, by the kind of effect associated, for us today, by the experience with Riemann's 1854 habilitation dissertation by such outstanding successors of Riemann as Planck, Einstein, and Vernadsky.

Riemann's work broke science free, in principle, from old, decrepit, a-priori assumptions, through the practical effects of working through the image of actually building our way outward, as if from within a pre-established, seemingly fixed scheme of the universe, into a conception of a universe which, in itself, expresses its role in a continuing process of upward, qualitative evolution in man's power to change the universe. Such had been the issue of Philo of Alexandria's condemnation of the Aristoteleans of his time. This was a development in man's knowledge which has been of a type roughly analogous to the evolution of the Solar system, beginning with the periodic table of the Sun itself, to a planetary form of Solar system with a higher order of elements, reaching beyond the traditional periodic table of D.I. Mendeleyev, and into the more recent so-called trans-uranic elements. This conclusion is no mere speculation; it is simply the quality of scientific fact which was unleashed, as it was for me, by the effects of following the trail from Riemann's 1854 habilitation dissertation.

The implications of that to which I have just pointed in the preceding paragraph, in particular, brings to our attention something which has always been there for man to recognize, but something which has been avoided out of respect for either the Aristotelean or kindred notions of a simply fixed order within creation.[9]

This power, which exists as typical of the prototype of the human individual, does not exist as a willful power in any other form of life, even though the principle of anti-entropic forms of upward biological evolution of species, shows the biological-evolutionary system to be under the rule of the anti-entropic principle also expressed in the biology of the Biosphere. Other living creatures are subsumed by that principle; *mankind, to be seen as subsumed by the Creator*, embodies that principle as its own.

These considerations are not speculative, but practical.

The only competent definition of creativity, is rejection of what is assumed to be a qualitatively fixed system of the universe, replacing that definition by the corrected notion of a universe being actively recreated, negentropically, in higher forms, that being under the control of an anti-entropic law of the universe as a whole.

The so-called "Second Law of Thermodynamics" is much worse than being, as it is, essentially, merely a fraud of Clausius, et al. There is no actual universal law of entropy in this universe, although there are, admittedly, as among academics, especially those in the train of the Liberal system of Paolo Sarpi, rather stupid doctrinaires who express a different opinion on the matter.

The preceding set of summary observations just stated by me here, is the conception subsumed by the fruit of the truly clinical evidence of the actual characteristics of human individual creativity, as in physical-scientific creativity, but also Classical modes of artistic creativity. Other living processes and their evolution, are subsumed by the universe as it exists as given to them; however, man is unique, as human creativity shows: unique in man's power to introduce principled changes into the universe, rather than simply obey them, when they occur. This is not some arbitrary assertion by me; it is the evidence of the increase of the human population on this planet, when the pattern of the human species' performance is contrasted to that of the higher apes.

---

9. In the time of Jesus Christ and his Apostles, the Aristoteleans of that time were arguing that, if God the Creator were a perfect being, he himself could not have changed the perfected universe once he had created it. The dogma of the modern Malthusian does not extend to be a law of nature, nor as of mankind's evolutionary potential. The perfection of the Creator, contrary to Aristotle, is the power to continue creating without limit. The entire universe shouts this fact as truth, except for the fools who have decided, arbitrarily to assert the contrary to be true and also eternal.

Defy the Children of Satan!

Given that background material summarized in this present chapter thus far, our attention should now be focused upon the psychopathological implications of the virtually cancerous mental disease, that modern syphilis of the human soul, called "environmentalism."

To wit, the ability of the human species to support a global population of about 6.7 billions persons, so vastly surpasses the population-potentials of the higher apes, qualitatively, that we must tend, even for that reason alone, toward recognizing, on the basis of such evidence, that the human population's characteristics are premised on mankind's creating its own needed environment to support increase of the human population-potential, per capita and per square kilometer. There is no naturally fixed upper limit on the human population's ability to reach far beyond present levels of its population on this planet. There are other questions to be asked and answered on this account, down the line, but those questions, themselves, are not, for us presently, of a quality relevant to the immediate prospects of mankind within the present century.

What we should know now, at least in an impressively large degree, are facts respecting the nature of the human potential which produces results of a type which are excluded among all other mammalian, or inferior species. These expressed differences all lie within the practical domain specific to true human mental creativity.

So, ask again: ***What Is Human Creativity?*** What, and who are the enemies of that human creativity?

So far, we have empirical access to knowledge of two specific types of experience of true creativity. First, we have local creativity, as by individual discoverers of practicable knowledge of provable universal principles. Second, there is knowledge of creativity as built into the essential character of the universe we inhabit, as the matter of the discovery of trans-uranic elements illustrates that point.

However, pause for a moment at this point: not *"How do we know this?"* but *"Why do we know this?"* Any among us who have thought seriously about *why discoveries of principle occur in a non-statistical way,* and who have actually made such discoveries successfully, will be able to understand the significance, and profound accuracy of my question: *"Why do we know this?"* The complementary question is, then: *"How do we know this?"* Name *"Why do we know this,"* ***Prometheus***, and *"How do we know this,"* ***Epimetheus***.

Why should we be able, and willing, to pose a valid question of a new principle, when that question has not been derived "logically," as a question, from preceding experience? In fact, so far in known history, most people are decidedly "not willing." Discovery of principle is not generated by experience; it is generated by the concern that we must abandon our habits, in order to go outside the mere repetition of existing experience. The inspiration we require, if we are to escape the monotonies of mere memory, lies not in experience as such, but in the imagination, as Percy B. Shelley, for example, presents the summation of this case in the concluding paragraph of his ***A Defence of Poetry***.[10]

This power of the imagination, to which Shelley refers in the conclusion of that book, is sometimes identified as the power of inductive, as opposed to deductive reasoning. However, not in the ordinary sense of the use of the term "inductive." The case of Kepler's uniquely original discovery of the harmonic character of the principle of universal gravitation, illustrates the case. In short, since we are confident that the universe is lawfully reasonable for the potential powers of the human mind, the evidence of a systemic paradox in evidence infuses us with confidence that systemic paradoxes in the reading of evidence have a solution, including the cases of systemic paradoxes

---

10. I quote here the relevant same passage from Shelley quoted as a footnote in my *Nations as Dynamical*: "...we live among such philosophers and poets as surpass beyond comparison any who have appeared since the last national struggle for civil and religious liberty. The most unfailing herald, companion, and follower of the awakening of a great people to work a beneficial change in opinion or institution, is poetry. At such periods, there is an accumulation of the power of communicating and receiving profound and impassioned conceptions respecting man and nature. The persons in whom this power resides, may often, as far as regards many portions of their nature, have little apparent correspondence with that spirit of good of which they are the ministers. But even whilst they deny and abjure, they are yet compelled to serve, the power which is seated upon the throne of their own soul. It is impossible to read the compositions of the most celebrated writers of the present day without being startled with the electric life which burns within their words. They measure the circumference and sound the depths of human nature with a comprehensive and all-penetrating spirit, and they are themselves perhaps the most sincerely astonished at its manifestations: for it is less their spirit than the spirit of the age. ..." That passage must be restated, in print and sung aloud, repeatedly, for the sake of its unique relevance as being uttered by me, yet once again, as stating a principle which is typical of every culture, in every age: that the individual member of society should become able to recognize himself, or herself, as expressing a behavior which is often, predominantly, typical of the movement of his, or her time, rather than simply a conscious product of his own, individual opinion-making. (My punctuation and editing.) Without that concluding paragraph of his *A Defence of Poetry*, any reprint of Shelley's piece were fraudulent by intent.

GNU Free Documentation License/Hamedog

There is no naturally fixed upper limit on the human population's ability to reach far beyond its present numbers, LaRouche says. Shown: a street in Hong Kong, one of the most densely populated places in the world.

expressed in our experience of the universe itself.

This quality of existence of confidence in the probable affinity of the human mind with the intention of the Creator, always lurks within our thinking, even if this appears only as a kind of last resort.

So, we are inspired, thus, to be alert to cases in which we mislead ourselves, or are otherwise misled, into assuming that some assumedly "self-evident" assumption will explain away reality, as this is typified by the case of the a-priori axioms and postulates of a Euclidean geometry. The very fact that we reject those a-prioristic presumptions alerts us to some great fallacy of assumption in our way of thinking about the relevant subject-matter.

Thus, the elimination of the *a-priori* notions of time and space, together, or respectively, typifies the existence of a dividing-line between true inductive reasoning and childish, a-prioristic presumptions respecting whatever reality is affected by this matter. Sometimes, the name for systemic forms of intellectual stupidity is called "being a practical person." Such a "practical person," like the typical follower of the empiricism of the followers of Paolo Sarpi, makes up all sorts of what are, in fact, lies, if that fiction appears to be an opinion which will be taken as convincing by the proverbial next, credulous sucker. The religious fanaticism of the self-righteously ignorant, is merely typical of this pathological syndrome.

Thus, like Plato, Nicholas of Cusa, Johannes Kepler, or Bernhard Riemann, all truly great scientists are theologians in the matter of fundamental scientific principles. Such is to be recognized in Albert Einstein in his later works, and in Academician V.I. Vernadsky. The method of thinking which inspires them is always a reflection of the ancient notion of *dynamis* on which Leibniz premised that concept of modern *dynamics* brought to its richer apprehension by Bernhard Riemann.

Such is the case of the paradox of human scientific reason.

In the case of human reason's achievements on behalf of mankind, when we are confronted with the evidence of truly creative modes of reasoning, as Shelley points toward this in the concluding paragraph of his ***A Defence of Poetry***, we encounter a phenomenon, thus, which we know, in one sense, as cognitive creative mentation in the individual. However, the action which that thinking by the individual extends into the form of intended changes in the way of thinking in society, and across the boundaries of death, into other parts of society, and coming generations, should warn us that the evidence thus presented to us has a more universal effect than a change in the behavior of that isolated individual. Thus, such creativity, as typified by the discovery of a universal physical principle, belongs ontologically to the domain of social dynamics, *universal* social dynamics. It thus becomes, as it grows, in effect, into an existent object among generations of mortals. It is, thus, the innermost part of the human personality which is efficiently immortal. It transmits its effect by a kind of mode of resonance, such that even when the idea originates within an individual mind, it reflects the dynamic action which that mind inhabits at that time; because of that arrangement, that aspect of the individual is itself immortal, and that dynamically.

Thus, the essential action of the thinking individual is the achievement of immortality of the self through that medium of action within and upon the immortal universe. It is probably the case, as I would attest from experience, that that sense of immortality, as we can readily recognize that in Shelley himself, and in his appreciation of John Keats, works exactly as Shelley himself describes this experience of his, in the concluding paragraph of his ***A Defence of Poetry***.

Awakening the True America:
Who Are the Coup Plotters Really?

by Michael G. Steger

Dec. 11—Have you ever been to West Virginia? The pro-Union state along the Ohio River in the hills of Appalachia, and not far from the nation's capital—the same West Virginia that was the iconic symbol of FDR's New Deal Presidency, and again of John Kennedy's? It is now the front line of the fight to return the U.S.A. to the American System of political economy and develop a nation of prosperity and growth once again. You didn't know?

While you were sleeping, West Virginia has agreed to $84 billion in investments in major manufacturing, materials, and mining, including state-of-the-art technologies, over the next twenty years. This is more than their annual GDP. It will end the opioid epidemic, the spiralling death rate, the unemployment crisis, and the general breakdown of the state and its five million citizens. Did Wall Street make this investment? You think maybe Goldman Sachs? Maybe it was the Federal Reserve?

Over the last ten years the Federal Reserve has loaned trillions of dollars to address the 2008 financial crisis. From 2009 to 2014, the Fed was lending on average nearly $50 billion a month to Wall Street banks. That is equivalent to $3 trillion over five years. In 2013, it was actually lending $85 billion a month to Wall Street banks. So, certainly it would find it easy to lend $85 billion to West Virginia over twenty years, or 240 months, for state-of-the-art manufacturing of petrochemicals for a growing global market. Not quite.

Wall Street and the Federal Reserve refuse to lend to West Virginia, or any other state, for long-term development. The Governor of West Virginia, Jim Justice, said at a recent press conference held to discuss the upcoming investments, that when he entered office earlier

EDITORIAL

this year, West Virginia was $500 million in debt, had "no rainy day" fund and had absolutely nowhere to turn.

Nowhere to turn? A state in the richest nation in the world? With the largest financial sector in history? After seven years of economic recovery? With nearly one trillion dollars in profits for Wall Street every year, above costs. And West Virginia has nowhere to turn?

Not surprisingly, the leading representative of the American System of political economy came to the rescue, with strong support from President Trump to make it happen. Was that the Oracle of Omaha, Warren Buffet? Bill Gates, or Jeff Bezos? If you guessed China, you've been paying attention.

China is the leading proponent of the American System of political economy on the planet, and this is the very secret to the success of China over the last thirty years. It has nothing to do with political party or political system. It is the commitment of government to employ the potential of the nation, through prudent control of the nation's system of credit, which is the defining factor for the development of the United States, West Virginia, every state of our Union, and every nation on our planet. China has demonstrated the universality of this system over the last thirty years, and Wall Street and its controllers in London are panicked.

You are now beginning to understand the coup plot against President Trump.

Now consider some of what's been in the news, but which requires more emphasis.

Over the recent weeks the Robert Mueller-run coup against President Trump has been thoroughly exposed as a British-instigated and Obama-orchestrated attack against what the British and Obama perceive as their political enemies among President Trump and his advisers. It started as early as 2014, with British surveillance against Trump associates, and reaches as high, and likely much higher than the Assistant Deputy Attorney General of the Obama Justice Department.

Assistant Deputy Attorney General Bruce G. Ohr is now known to have had direct contact with British spy Christopher Steele during the summer of 2016 regarding his British-concocted dodgy dossier, which was paid for by Hillary Clinton, Obama, and likely the FBI. Ohr's wife, Nellie H. Ohr, worked for Fusion GPS, which passed the money to Steele for his dossier. This dossier, as many now know, was then used to open an investigation against Trump and his associates, and was likely used to justify the unconstitutional "unmasking" of Trump associates during a Presidential election. If Bruce Ohr knew, did Attorney General Loretta Lynch know? Did National Security Director, and infamous unmasker Susan Rice know? Did then President Obama know, and did he then sign the Foreign Intelligence Surveillance Act (FISA) warrants for wiretapping his political opponents, based on a report of trashy unverified lies, compiled by British intelligence and paid for by the Hillary Clinton Campaign, Obama's campaign organization, and potentially Obama's FBI?

All of these questions are now at the forefront of numerous Congressional investigations, in effect, judoing the Russian collusion story into an investigation of high-level, Nazi-like abuse of the federal government through the Obama Administration's collusion with British intelligence in an attempt to prevent, and then undermine the fair election of President Trump. (See Will Wertz' article in this issue.)

However sparse the coverage of this story in the mainstream press, it is just the immediate plot. The conspiracy is much deeper. And on this broader conspiracy, *EIR* has published an in-depth report known as the *Mueller Dossier*, which exposes the specific role of Robert Mueller as a legal thug-assassin, operating for decades on behalf of the very same British group at the center of the operation against Donald Trump.

In quick summary, as related to the main subject of this editorial, the Mueller Dossier documents the very hand of the FBI/DOJ, via hit-men such as Mueller, as the instrument of British attacks against any political threat to British control of the American political system and—what is the main subject of this report—the American financial and economic system. The Mueller Dossier begins with the British-directed attack on Lyndon LaRouche and his organization starting in the early 1980s, when LaRouche was personally working with national security officials of the Reagan administration on what eventually became the Strategic Defense Initiative (SDI). It then covers Mueller's and the FBI's major role in the cover-up of the Sept. 11, 2001 terrorist attacks, as well as the ongoing orchestrated attack against President Donald Trump by the Obama apparatus. The British role, and Mueller's personal role as a British enforcer, could not be more clear in all of these operations to undermine and ultimately control the U.S. political process.

Read the Mueller Dossier in full to get the true story of American politics over the last 30 years.

This story will continue to unfold over the coming weeks, even finding its way into the press as the Congressional investigations pursue these leads.

What's Not in the News

Now, consider what's not even mentioned in the news.

Did you know there is an even more sensational story about to dominate all of the international headlines, one that everyone knows about, even while no one is talking about it publicly? Need a hint? Consider the deeper enemies of the U.S.A. which control the FBI and would rather destroy the United States than lose their political control.

For perspective, consider the creation of the FBI in the early part of the 20th Century by Anglophile President Teddy Roosevelt. His uncle, James Dunwoody Bulloch, was the head of Confederate Intelligence in London, and his Attorney General, Charles Bonaparte, established the FBI in 1908, ostensibly in response to the assassination of pro-American System President William McKinley. Not unlike the attempted assassination of President Reagan 80 years later, which was orchestrated by forces supporting George H.W. Bush, the assassination of President McKinley in 1901 was intended to bring to power not simply rough-riding Teddy, but the British forces which controlled him.

Once the FBI was established as a federal police force, essentially unchecked by Congress (whom they would easily blackmail), the FBI was deployed to attack the strength of the U.S.-German ties that had developed between President Grant and Chancellor Bismarck during the industrial revolution, as well as the legacy of German culture of such as Beethoven, Mozart, and

Schiller, who were well-known throughout all of the cities of the United States, and especially in cultural centers such as Manhattan and Chicago. (U.S.-Russian ties were also attacked. They had prospered prior to the 1905 and 1917 revolutions with the development of the trans-Siberian railway, which was modeled on our transcontinental system.) This attack against U.S.-German relations would help make possible both World Wars and their devastation.

Under the presidencies of Anglophiles Teddy Roosevelt and then Woodrow Wilson, Wall Street took over total control of the United States banking system, including the creation of national debt and the restriction on national credit through the Wall Street-dominated Federal Reserve System.

Fortunately for the nation, in 1933, President Franklin Roosevelt, who had broken from his family's political tradition, re-established the American System of banking and credit that Presidents Lincoln and Grant had successfully employed to create the industrial revolution. FDR, by moving against what he called the "moneychangers in the Temple" referring to Wall Street, kept FBI Director J. Edgar Hoover and his band of cultural degenerates at bay, as he prepared the nation for war. However, soon after FDR's death, British assets such as J. Edgar Hoover, under the small-minded President Truman, re-established British control over both the political system, via the Cold War, as well as over the system of national credit FDR had initiated.

Though President Eisenhower was capable of withstanding the pressures against him, as we saw with his intervention to defend Egypt's control of the Suez Canal, and also with his interstate highway system, he acknowledged the British takeover in his farewell address in 1961, warning the nation of the political power the pro-British faction had imposed on the U.S.A. since the end of World War II, which he named the "Military-Industrial Complex."

Because of this British imposition, President Kennedy was to suffer a very different fate.

President John Kennedy, who like FDR broke from his family's political class, had committed himself to re-establishing the American System of political economy that FDR had revived. His commitment to a manned mission to the Moon, and its later, posthumous, unparalleled success, demonstrate President Kennedy's scientific understanding of the American System. That is, that through shared scientific advancement and industrial development, as seen in the space program, in nuclear power, and in water development in the western states, all problems both foreign and domestic could be resolved towards peace and collaboration. President Reagan's SDI echoed this same principle two decades later.

The British and pro-British plotters who premised their power and success on the destruction of the American System—the very system by which we had gained our independence and become the unrivaled economic power on the planet—recognized the threat of President Kennedy's American System policy. Perhaps most important, through Kennedy's commitment to long-term deep space exploration, his encouragement of science and scientific discovery among all walks of American life, and the accompanying industrial benefits for all nations, Kennedy not only posed an existential threat to British control over U.S. policy, but to the very existence of the British system and its culture globally.

For the forces aligned with the British system and facing this existential threat, nothing was too risky if it would end the American System policy of President Kennedy. As we have seen with previous American heroes such as Alexander Hamilton, who was killed by British agent and traitor Aaron Burr, or President Lincoln, killed by a British coup-plot planned from Montreal, or with President McKinley, this British system and its intelligence and police agents will kill our greatest leaders, either physically or legally, and by any means possible.

When President Kennedy's body was flown from Dallas back to Andrews Air Force Base outside Washington, D.C., his brother Bobby, family, and other friends gathered to await the plane. One of those friends was Congressman Neil Gallagher of New Jersey. In a 2013 interview available on YouTube conducted by LaRouche PAC, Rep. Gallagher says in his own words, that he saw Bobby Kennedy pacing back and forth near a bus on the far side of the hangar. When he walked over to him, Bobby looked up and said, "That goddamn Hoover did it!"

This is the British control of the FBI, and all to enforce British-directed economic and geopolitical policy.

A similar attack was run against President Reagan. George H.W. Bush was supposed to be the 1980 GOP nominee—like "low energy Jeb" in 2016—not the upstart actor from California. Yet President Reagan was the best President in a generation, and had he not been nearly assassinated less than 100 days into office, he would have had an even more profound effect on our nation, likely returning us back to the program of industry and science that his team from California recognized, and on which they consulted with Lyndon LaRouche and his associates, who were the leading representatives of the American System then, as now.

Soon after the attempt on Reagan's life, the Bush League with explicit direction from London, deployed the FBI and DOJ ostensibly to exterminate LaRouche and his movement. Their attack dog was Robert Mueller.

This is the FBI. This is Mueller. This is what underlies Mueller's and Obama's rabid hatred of Trump and this nation. This is the British deployment time and time again, against our beloved country. And this is the intent against President Trump.

It is a philosophical and scientific distinction, as well as a deeply held religious view of man, which separates true Patriots from British-directed traitors such as Mueller, Obama, or the satanic George Soros.

Our current Wall Street system of speculation is premised on the axiom that man is simply a beast-like creature, motivated by individual hedonistic desires, who must be controlled, and at times culled. The intended result is an economic system which benefits only the Wall Street feudalist class, looting the population with massive increases in ground rent, with stock bubbles, and with black market cash-based commodities like narcotics and human trafficking. If continued, this British system would eliminate all aspects of advanced manufacturing, infrastructure development, and space exploration, and in doing so, reduce the United States and world population to a small class of doped-up modern serfs, using smartphones and social networking to better provide obedient service to our British-inspired oligarchs. Unless, of course, the resulting political instability leads to nuclear war first.

China today is developing and its population is growing, both in quality and quantity. Russia has a growing population today, for the first time in twenty-five years. This New Paradigm of growth is now spreading to all of Asia, including Southwest Asia, Africa, and even South America. To the British System, and its financiers, this is unacceptable—and if it cannot be stopped by any other means, then war is inevitable, even nuclear war. This was the Obama policy, and it is nothing less than satanic.

Thus, the solution to end the Mueller-run coup against President Trump is an immediate return to the principles of Alexander Hamilton's American System. (See LaRouche's Four New Laws as a policy directive to implement the American System.) It is the question of the American System, a system of development premised on the principles developed during the flourishing culture of the Florentine Renaissance, a culture based on the idea of man created in the image of a loving creator, who to be successful must "be fruitful and multiply." This was the cultural starting point for the development of the United States and the early colonies, which came to be known as the American System via Hamilton's development of national banking, public credit, and investments in manufacturing and the powers of labor, land development, and national infrastructure platforms.

This is the question of national credit, directed by the President and Congress for large-scale national infrastructure platforms which raise the productivity of the entire nation. Never credit for Wall Street speculation. Their speculation is made possible—as we see from the bailouts of $85 billion per month—only by the trillions of dollars of U.S. public debt created by and under the control of Wall Street and their London backers, who depend on the ongoing submission by our fellow Americans.

Rare moments in history arise, in which the political forces of these two systems become as clear as they are now. Decisive action from fellow Americans, as well as Universal Patriots, has never been more required.

It is time once again to return to the beneficial policies of the American System, set forth for the modern era by leading American System economist Lyndon LaRouche.

This is the political fight we must win.